SASSANIAN ARMIES

The Iranian Empire
early 3rd to mid-7th centuries AD

Dr. David Nicolle

Colour Plates
by
Angus McBride

Published by Montvert Publications

Published in 1996 by Montvert Publications

© Copyright 1996 Montvert Publications

Montvert Publications, 2 Kingswood Grove, Reddish, Stockport SK5 6SP

Montvert Publications (Distribution), PO Box 25, Stockport SK5 6RU

ISBN 1 874101 08 6

A CIP catalogue record for this book is available from the British Library.

Printed by Joseph Ward Colourprint Ltd. Dewsbury, Yorkshire

A note to the reader: this is one of a series of Montvert titles which aim to present some of the best up to date analyses of the history, dress, equipment and organization of various ancient and medieval armies.
Dr. Philip Greenough (editor)

In this book the black&white figures have been interleaved with the main text for aesthetic reasons. They should certainly not, however, be regarded just as 'filling'. They should be regarded as an integral and vital part of the book and and they deliberately have been given much longer accompanying captions than those typical of other books of comparable size. We hope the reader will appreciate the extra information contained therein.

Introduction

The Sassanian Empire was the last in a series of Persian empires which had for centuries been seen as the rivals of Graeco-Roman civilization. It was also the last before the coming of Islam changed the entire character of Persian or Iranian civilization. In many ways the Sassanian Empire already had one foot in this new medieval world, yet its self-image was firmly cast in the mould of ancient Iran and the Empire regarded itself as the true heir of that great Achaemenid Persian Empire destroyed by Alexander the Great hundreds of years earlier.

In some ways Sassanian Iran also had more in common with Hindu India than subsequent Muslim Iran. People were divided into "castes" with an Iranian warrior elite of supposed "Aryan" origin dominating others of inferior birth. The domain of the Shahanshah or Sassanian King of Kings become identified with Iranshahr, the Land of the Iranians and of the Zoroastrian religion. There were many Iranians outside the Sassanian Empire and many non-Iranians within, yet this ethnically based attitude was deep rooted and would, to some extent, even survive the egalitarian spirit of Islam. Like their Roman rivals the Sassanian Iranians were trapped within an archaic view of the world. While the Romans believed that they were the natural masters of civilization, the Iranians believed that their King was the divinely ordained master of all kings.

Meanwhile the real world was changing fast and both empires faced potentially mortal threats from the Turco-Mongol nomadic peoples of Central Asia. The Sassanian Shahanshah recognized this more clearly than the Roman Emperor and often attempted a joint effort against the common foe. Yet even the Shahanshah was hampered by deep anti-Roman antagonism among his own warrior nobility and particularly among the Zoroastrian priestly caste.

Despite large-scale conversion to Christianity in the final century, Zoroastrianism and its *Mobad* priests were too deeply entrenched for the Sassanian state to have become Christian. Then a new threat erupted from an unexpected direction. This was the Muslim Arab invasion which in only fifteen years crushed what had been seen as the most powerful Empire in western Asia.

The Sassanian Dynasty & Historical Outline

199 AD   Roman army sacks Parthian capital at Ctesiphon.

217 AD   Peace between Parthians & Roman Empire.

220 AD   Revolt of Ardashir, first of the Sassanians.

226 AD   Defeat & death of last of the Parthian rulers; Ardashir I proclaimed Emperor of Iran.

232 AD   Ardashir I makes peace with Rome; Sassanians annex Armenia.

241 AD   Sassanians invade Syria.

260 AD   Sassanians capture of Roman Emperor Valerian.

263 AD   Palmyrene Arabs defeat Shapur I.

283 AD   Romans seize Sassanian capital of Ctesiphon, then retreat.

286 AD   Tiradates seizes Armenia.

297 AD   Romans defeat Narseh; Sassanians abandon provinces west of Tigris.

338 AD   Shapur II besieges Roman-held Nisibis.

348 AD   Shapur II invades Roman Mesopotamia.

363 AD   Romans invade Iran; are defeat; Sassanians re-occupy western provinces plus Nisibis.

376 AD   Peace between Romans & Sassanians.

410 AD   Council of Seleucia; Alaric the Goth takes Rome.

421 AD   Peace between Sassanians & Romans.

425 AD   First raids by Ephthalites (White Huns) into Sassanian Empire.

455 AD   Vandals sack Rome.

483 AD   Peroz defeated by Ephthalites.

488 AD   Sassanian campaign against Khazars.

513 AD   End of Ephthalite raids.

524 AD   War between Sassanians & Byzantines.

529 AD   Byzantine Emperor closes School of Athens; Greek scholars flee to Sassanian Empire.

531 AD   Sassanians defeated by Byzantines at Callinicum.

533 AD   Peace between Sassanians & Byzantines.

540 AD   Sassanians invade Syria, sack Antioch.

562 AD   Second peace between Sassanians & Byzantines.

570 AD   (circa) Sassanians conquer Yemen.

590 AD   Revolt of Varahran Chobin.

603 AD   War between Sassanians & Byzantines.

614 AD   Sassanians conquer Syria, occupy Jerusalem, carry off "True Cross".

617 AD   Sassanians occupy much of Byzantine Anatolia.

622 AD   Byzantine Emperor defeats Sassanians; begins reconquest of Middle East. Prophet Muhammad establishes first Muslim community in Madina.

627 AD   Byzantines invade Iran.

628 AD   Start of civil war in Iran.

632 AD   Death of Prophet Muhammad in Arabia.

635 AD   Muslim Arabs take Damascus from Byzantines.

636 AD   Muslim Arabs defeat Byzantines at Battle of Yarmuk in Syria & Sassanians at battle of Qadisiyah in Iraq.

637 AD   Muslim Arabs seize Sassanian capital at Ctesiphon.

642 AD   Muslim Arab crush Sassanian army at Nahavand; conquer Persia.

651 AD   Death of last recognized Sassanian Emperor Yazdagird III; end of the Sassanian Empire.

The Sassanian Dynasty

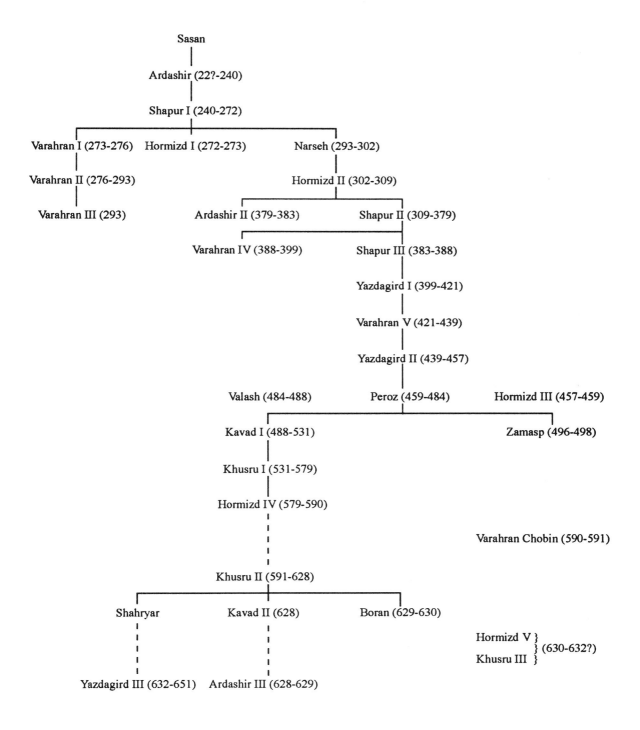

Sasan

Ardashir (22?-240)

Shapur I (240-272)

Varahran I (273-276)   Hormizd I (272-273)   Narseh (293-302)

Varahran II (276-293)   Hormizd II (302-309)

Varahran III (293)   Ardashir II (379-383)   Shapur II (309-379)

Varahran IV (388-399)   Shapur III (383-388)

Yazdagird I (399-421)

Varahran V (421-439)

Yazdagird II (439-457)

Valash (484-488)   Peroz (459-484)   Hormizd III (457-459)

Kavad I (488-531)   Zamasp (496-498)

Khusru I (531-579)

Hormizd IV (579-590)

Varahran Chobin (590-591)

Khusru II (591-628)

Shahryar   Kavad II (628)   Boran (629-630)

Hormizd V }
          } (630-632?)
Khusru III }

Yazdagird III (632-651)   Ardashir III (628-629)

The Character of the Sassanian Empire

Though the Sassanians modelled themselves on the ancient Achaemenid Persian Empire, their state was really very different. Like Rome the Sassanian Empire relied heavily on slave labour, but at the same time Sassanian merchants ranged far and wide, gradually ousting the Romans from the lucrative Indian Ocean trade routes. It was also a time of increased metallurgical production so that Iran earned a somewhat undeserved reputation as the "armoury of Asia". In fact the main Sassanian mining centres were on the fringes of the Empire, in Armenia, the Caucusus and above all Transoxania. The extraordinary mineral wealth of the Pamir mountains on the eastern horizon of the Sassanian Empire led to a legend among the Iranian-speaking Tajiks which is still told today. It was said that when God was making the world he tripped over the Pamirs, dropping his jar of minerals which spread across the region.

At the heart of the Sassanian Empire sat the Emperor - a figure of huge power and prestige. The previous Parthian dynasty, which drove Alexander the Great's successors out of Iran, had adopted a Hellenistic Greeks deification of kingship. This, when added to ancient Iranian cults, placed the ruler between heaven and earth as a link between his subjects and the great god Ahura Mazda. Around the ruler stood his family, held together by clan loyalty and ancestor veneration. No Sassanian books on government have survived but the 9th century "Book of the Crown" is based on a Sassanian prototype. It emphasizes the splendour of a Divinely ordained ruler, the passivity of his subjects, and makes very few concessions to concepts of justice, generosity and compassion. Such abstract ideas had to await a later series of Muslim Persian and Arabic "Mirrors for Princes".

Although the collapse of the Sassanian Empire was sudden and unexpected the Sassanian heritage remained important in Iran, if not always beneficial. The early 7th century saw defeat in a war of epic proportions against the Romano-Byzantines. From a Mediterranean perspective this conflict marked the true "end of antiquity". For Iran it paved the way for the Muslim Arabs to make the first successful invasion from the west since the days of Alexander the Great.

Paradoxically, perhaps, this crushing of the Sassanians led to what has been described as "The Golden Age of Persia". It would also see eastern and western Iran truly united for the first time in history. Some aspects of Sassanian civilization would survive in Semirechye, south of Lake Balkash, as late as the 12th century. Meanwhile the brilliant civilization of Classical Islam, the world of the Caliphs as still recalled in the legendary "Thousand and One Nights", owed a great deal to its Sassanian predecessor. This was particularly true in military matters . The first Arabic book on tactics and army organization is believed to have been a translation, now lost, of a Persian work written for Ardashir back in the 3rd century AD.

The Parthian Background

The Parthians who overthrew the Seleucid successors of Alexander were nomads from what is now Turkmenistan. Though Iranian-speakers they were never accepted as legitimate successors of the lost Achaemenids by the Persians of western Iran. Their horse-archery tactics, including the famous "Parthian shot", had more in common with Central Asia than the rest of Iran where archery had previously been an infantry affair. After defeating the Seleucids the Parthians tried to re-employ Hellenistic infantry, heavy and light, but these were unreliable so the Parthians reverted to Iranian cavalry traditions while adding their own horse-archery skills. Basic Parthian tactics normally began with a charge by heavy cavalry to clear away enemy light horsemen. Parthian horse-archers would then shoot at the now bunched up enemy infantry.

Such tactics used huge numbers of arrows and here the Parthians had a system of baggage camels to re-supply their archers during a battle. To use a bow effectively on horseback also demands great riding skill which was mostly to be found among nomads. The fully developed composite bow was, however, a formidable weapon with good penetration up to 100 metres and an effective harrassing range of 250 metres. The Parthians still employed large numbers of infantry particularly when fighting in mountainous terrain, but only a small part of the army was actually under the direct control of the king. It also seems likely that a

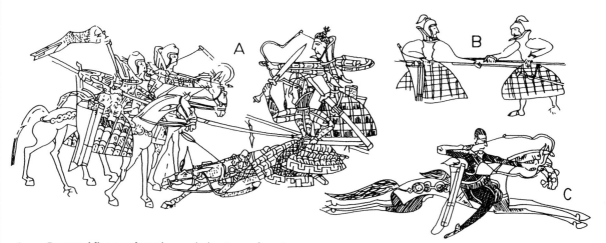

1.   Engraved figures of warriors and a huntsman from two decorated bronze belt plaques (A & C) plus a bronze strap-end (B) from Kurgan-Tepe; Sughdian Parthian 2nd to 1st centuries BC.

A   On the left two armoured horsemen, one with a heavy spear and the other with a composite bow, attack enemy figures, one of whom appears to be rising from his fallen horse. The horse has been shot in the neck by an arrow. All these warriors are armed and armoured in much the same way except that one has lost his helmet. The most notable features of their equipment are vertically overlapping lamellar cuirasses with very tall collars, helmets which also cover the sides and rear of the neck, very large spears, long straight and double-edged swords, angled form of composite bows, and the fact that two archers carry both quivers and bowcases on their right hips. With the exception of this perhaps archaic way of carrying archery equipment, most would persist throughout the subsequent Sassanian Empire and well into the Islamic period.

B   A pair of more simply drawn infantry warriors fight with spears. They come from a decorated strap-end. Apart from the plumes in their helmets the only major difference is that they appear to wear jackets over the upper part of their armours.

C   This vigorous but stylized representation of a horse-archer is part of a group pursuing wild rams, onagers, etc. Like the other horsemen he rides without stirrups while the horse's bridle has substantial psalions or cheek-pieces on each side of the bit. It is interesting to note that whereas the bow-cases of every warrior, whether on horseback or on foot, are of a type which holds a ready-strung weapon, the huntsman's bowcase is of a narrower form to carry an unstrung weapon. This might suggest that it was more important for a soldier to carry his weapon ready for immediate use, whereas this was not necessary for a hunter. On the other hand there was little consistency in such a use of bowcases over subsequent centuries, nor indeed between one region and another. Composite bows also retain their strength better when kept strung whereas simple wooden bows are better if stored unstrung. (location unknown).

D   Reconstruction of an early Parthian warrior based upon the decorated belt plaques from Kurgan-Tepe.

2.   Parthians.

A   Relief carving on a rock showing a warrior on an armoured horse, Parthian, c.200 AD. The horseman is so damaged that only a few features can be distinguished. Among them is a bushy hair-style which became characteristic of the Parthian warrior elite and would be copied in other parts of the Middle East. Another is a two-handed lance technique without a shield that had been used by most cavalrymen throughout Europe and the Middle East since Late Hellenistic times. It was probably of Central Asian origin, like most developments in horse-harness and cavalry warfare, and would continue to be used in the Middle East throughout the Middle Ages. The pattern on the rider's leg might indicate mail or some other form of armour but is more likely to represent the patterned cloth of very full trousers or the loose folds typical of Parthian riding gear. The horse is in better condition. Its armour is in two different styles, one for the body and the other for the neck, though both appear to be lamellar. Similarly dated horse-armours found in the Syrian Roman frontier fortress of Dura Europos were similarly in two distinct parts. The animal's body armour consisted of sheets of iron or bronze scales while another sheet of hardened leather lamellar probably protected its neck. Note that in this carving the warrior's quiver and long slender bowcase for an unstrung bow are almost certainly hung from the right rear of the saddle rather than the man's belt (in situ Tang-i Sarvak, Iran).

B Another equally damaged but simpler rock-relief carving from the same period shows a Parthian cavalryman thrusting his spear with one arm, almost in a medieval "couched lance" manner. He has a pointed hat or helmet and wears two belts, one perhaps supporting a bowcase or quiver which, on this occasion, does not seem to be attached to the saddle. The horse is clearly unarmoured (in situ Tang-i Sarvak, Iran).

C Stucco plaque of a saddled horse, Parthian or early Sassanian, 3rd century southern Iran. The remarkably large saddle-blanket on this horse may be a rudimentary form of quilted horse armour. It has similarities with the Parthian horse armour at Tang-i Sarvak (above) and with horse barding seen in slightly later Sassanian sources (British Museum, London).

D Stucco plaque, undated Parthian. Several typically Parthian characteristics can be seen in this virtually undamaged piece of stucco: the bushy hair of the Parthian military elite, a large cloak billowing out behind, a very loose-fitting shirt with a relatively short skirt as seen in the Roman World but rarely in the Sassanian Empire, and very loose-fitting trousers or leggings. This latter garment is illustrated in far greater detail in the art of Parthian-influenced Palmyra in Syria. The large circular medallions decorating the horse's breast and breeching straps would remain a feature of Iranian horse harness during the following Sassanian period (Louvre Museum, Paris).

E Terracotta ceramic plaque of a hunting scene, undated Parthian. This rather crude piece of art again shows the classic two-handed spear thrusting technique, while the horse clearly has a substantial curb bit with large cheek-pieces on each side of its mouth. The man's peculiar headgear is probably a hat worn over a helmet, a typical Iranian or Central Asian practice. There appears to be a mail aventail hanging beneath this hat. The most interesting aspect of the terracotta is, however, a large Central Asian form of lamellar cuirass. This hangs down to the lower legs but, again in typical Central Asian style, lacks any sleeves (British Museum, London).

F Terracotta plaque of a horse-archer, undated Parthian. This horseman is unarmoured but wears a tall cap, a short jacket and baggy trousers. His bow-case or quiver may hang from the saddle or from a waist belt. The similarity between this man's action and that shown on the engraved early Parthian belt decoration from Kurgan-Tepe is striking, although the style of art could hardly be more different (British Museum, London).

four-way division of the state, as used by the Sassanians, dated from Parthian times.

Experiments with horse-armour may first have been made in Khwarazm, south of the Aral Sea, during the early Iron Age and this province continued to serve as a point of contact between the armour traditions of Europe, western Asia and China during the Parthian period. Mail gives little defence against archery, and scale armour was now the preferred protection for man and horse. By the 3rd century AD, as the Parthians declined and the Sassanians emerged, there was also a shift from bronze to iron armour, and subsequently also to lamellar rather than scale. Lamellar offered the best resistance to arrows throughout the Middle Ages and a lamellar cuirass was a complex piece of equipment. The discovery of one-piece iron helmets in 8th century Transoxanian and perhaps even in 1st century north-western Indian archaeological sites indicates that these areas were superior to Europe in metallurgy, a technological superiority perhaps originally resulting from contacts with China. This similarly enabled the cavalrymen of Iran, Transoxania and what is now Afghanistan to wield iron swords longer than those seen in the West, blades 35.5 cms long and 5.25 cms broad probably being typical.

This superiority in horse-harness technology in the area referred to above may have been even greater. The nomadic Iranian Sarmatians of the western steppes (Ukraine and southern Russia) seem to have had saddles with rudimentary wooden "trees" or frames by the 1st century AD. This replaced the padded "blanket" form used elsewhere. The Sarmatians fought, however, with spears rather than bows and the new framed saddle was perhaps more important to a lancer than a horse-archer. Meanwhile the Parthians clearly had enormous military influence beyond their own frontiers. In the Middle East the Romans recruited Parthian deserters to fight in Iranian style while the elite of local armies such as those of Hatra and Palmyra tried to copy the Parthians in any way they could. This entire military tradition was then inherited by the Sassanians in the early 3rd century AD.

Sassanian Government & Military Organization

Sassanian society was highly complex with many nomadic people living within the Empire and having a separate tribal organization. Some of the previously dominant Parthian clans also remained important. Nevertheless the Empire was dominated by a small group of Persian noble families. The *marzban* provincial governors were drawn from their ranks, those of greatest seniority being permitted a silver throne while the *marzban* of the strategic Caucasus frontier was allowed a golden throne. Sassanian society was strictly divided into *azatan* "free men" who jealously guarded their status as descendants of the ancient Aryan conquerors and the mass of originally non-Aryan peasantry. These *azatan* formed a numerous minor aristocracy of lower ranking administrators, mostly living on their own small estates and providing the cavalry backbone of the Sassanian army. Of these the most prestigious were the armoured *aswaran* who normally decided the outcome of a battle.

The division of the cavalry into a heavy cavalry elite and a larger number of unarmoured horsemen first appeared in Iraq and western Iran in the Parthian period. It was done for ecological as well as cultural and social reasons. During the early Sassanian centuries there was a gradual downgrading of independently recruited cavalry in favour of those maintained by great barons. Not until the 6th century did the independant freeholding cavalry see a revival. By then the *dihqans* or minor gentry had been reduced to little more than a local defensive role. Nevertheless the old theory that warfare was the responsibility of the "Aryan" elite remained the ideal though in reality, of course, the "non-Aryan" low caste peasantry suffered as much as anyone.

At the centre of the Sassanian caste system was the Shahanshah King of Kings ruling over sub-kings, princes and powerful nobles. But the relatively independent sub-kings of the Parthian period were now fewer in number and were gradually replaced by Sassanian princes acting as provincial governors. The Imperial Court was at Ctesiphon (more accurately *Tyspwn* in Middle Persian) south of modern Baghdad

3. The crowns of early Sassanian rulers.

Each Sassanian King of Kings had his own elaborate form of headgear in which he was illustrated on coins and in triumphal art. Until the early 5th century these crowns varied a great deal, but from then on there were only minor changes until the last few Sassanian rulers began using highly individual crowns once again. Presumably these crowns would also have been worn on ceremonial occasions and perhaps even in war as a way of demonstrating the King of King's glory. These example are all taken from Sassanian rock-relief carvings at Naqsh-i Rajab, Naqsh-i Rustam, Bishapur, Sarab-i Bahram, Sar Mashhad and Taq-i Bustan.

A & B Ardashir I

C   Shapur I

D   Varahran I

E - H Varahran II

I   Narseh

J   Hormizd II

K   Shapur II

L   Shapur III

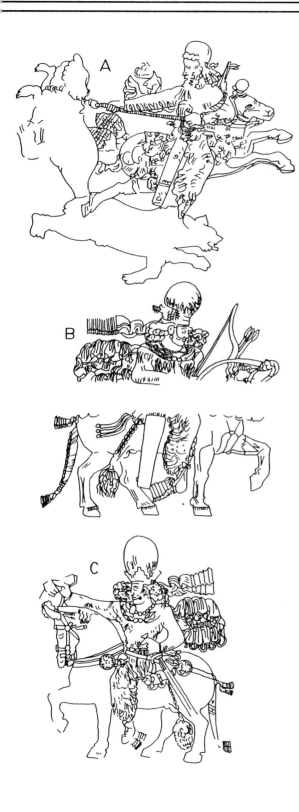

4. Sassanian art is dominated by images of the ruling King of Kings, Sassanian society being among the most monarchist the world has ever known. He was portrayed as the all-conquering hero, overthrowing enemies and wild beasts alike. He also represented a semi-divine individual standing between his subjects and the heavens above. This Iranian concept of society collapsed before the Muslims in the 7th century but gradually re-emerged during the following years to corrupt the egalitarian character of Arab Islam.

A Gilded silver plate showing Varahran I hunting bears, Sassanian 3rd century AD. On this occasion Varahran wears a simple form of headgear though it still has the main features of his his crown. Other royal or high aristocratic decorations are a pompom between the horse's ears and large tassles hanging from the rear of its harness. The ruler himself wears the loose shirt and trousers of a typical Sassanian horseman. He carries a bow over his left shoulder and a long tube-like quiver from a belt on his right hip. But the most striking feature of this plate is the fact that Varahran is using a lassoo to catch a bear. The lassoo was a Central Asian hunting device which could also be used in warfare, as it would be some centuries later in the Turco-Islamic Middle East (Abkhazian State Museum, Sukhumi, Georgia).

B Rock-relief carving of Varahran II, Sassanian late 3rd century AD. In this typical illustration of an all-conquering Sassanian ruler, he wears a winged crown with a great padded sphere on top and long streamers at the back. In addition to ear-rings and a jewelled necklace, the ruler's full beard has been tied into a tassle. His costume consists of the usual full shirt and baggy trousers with a long cape fastened across his chest by a clasp. The very long ribbons from a bow on top of his shoe are another feature of Sassanian aristocratic costume. Various tassles and ribbons dangle from the horse's harness and the animal's mane is decoratively trimmed. While a long vertical quiver hangs on the ruler's right hip, he carries a bow and three arrows in his left hand. It is interesting to note that this essentially Persian rather than Turkish style of archery survived until the 12th century when a military manual written for the Saladin himself recommended holding three arrows in the same hand as a bow. (in situ, Bishapur, Iran).

C Rock-relief carving of the Triumph of Shapur I, Sassanian mid-3rd century AD. This less damaged carving shows the King of Kings with captured Roman leaders, one man's sleeves being grasped by Shapur. Though his crown is different, this Sassanian ruler's costume is essentially the same as that worn by Varahran II at Bishapur, even down to his knotted beard. The undamaged central part of the carving shows several important features of Sassanian cavalry equipment, such as one of the "horns" at the front of the saddle which curves back over the rider's thigh. Also a suspender strap which supports a loose fabric legging, the doubled fastening or buckle of a waist-belt, a separate sword belt which goes through a slide on the scabbard, and the fact that the rider is armed with a very long straight-bladed sword. The horse's bridle has an early form of snaffle bit with broad psalions or cheek-pieces (in situ, Naqsh-i Rustam, Iran).

5. Cavalry elite in battle.

A Sassanian heavy cavalry overthrow their enemies, late 3rd or early 4th centuries AD. These four figures may represent Varahran II (upper left) and his son (lower left) defeating foreign and domestic foes. Both victorious riders appear to wield their lances using the two-handed techniques whereas at least one of their enemies does not. Three horses wear horse-armours of fabric-covered felt or perhaps merely decorative caparisons. These again would remain in use throughout the medieval period in Iran and some neighbouring countries. Note the length of the sword carried by the defeated lower right-hand figure. None of these cavalrymen carry shields, which were impractical with the two-handed lance technique (in situ, Naqsh-i Rustam, Iran).

B & C Sassanian "knights", rock relief carving of the Triumph of Shapur I over a Roman Emperor, late 3rd century AD. These are only some of a host of horsemen who salute their victorious ruler. Each figure is virtually identical, wearing the standard dress of the Persian cavalry elite, but their hats differ. All are basically of the *qalansuwa* type which continued to be used throughout the Middle Ages. Some even have padded animal shapes, suggesting that such headgear, whether or not worn over a helmet, served as a form of distinguishing mark (in situ, Bishapur, Iran).

in Iraq. It was known as the Heart of Iranshahr and consisted of seven towns forming one great metropolis.

Military affairs were in the hands of a small group of royal councellors. The *Vuzurg Framadar* or Great Commander acted as a Prime Minister. There were also many lesser *framadars* at Court, all of whom probably had some kind of military duties. In the early years the main *marzban* military regions were Armenia, Beth Aramaie in Iraq, Fars, Kirman, Isfahan, Azarbayjan, Tabaristan, Nishapur, Tus and Sijistan in Iran, Bahrayn in Arabia, Herat, Marw and

Serakhs in the east. Some were quite small, othe enjoyed considerable autonomy while certain are were militarily more important than others. Southe Azerbayjan facing the Caucasus was, for example, special frontier province under a specifically milita governorship while the eastern Caucasus frontier zo with its mixed population of Armenians, Kurds a Persians was similarly under a military governe South of the Caspian Sea and north of the Dasht Kavir salt desert the region around Rayy formed vital corridor linking the western Iranian heartlan with Khurasan in the east. The flexible boundari of Khurasan, the "Land of the Rising Sun", reflected the changing power of the Empire and its eastern rivals. Here the term *kanarang* was used instead of *marzban*, another example of how eastern and western Iran differed. In some places another title, *padgospan*, seems to have been used for a specifically military governor perhaps lacking civilian duties. The function of a *marzban* also changed over the years. Smaller territorial units were essentially part of the civil administration. At first the smallest of these was called *Shahr* with a *Shahristan* town at its centre and a *Shahrigh* selected from the local *dihqan* gentry in charge. In later years the *Shahrs* were divided into *Kuras*, and these into *rustaqs* or *tasug*. A *rustaq* was normally an irrigated rural area or oasis, often with a landowner's castle in the centre. This sophisticated structure was inherited by medieval Islamic civilization along with the Sassanian the *parvanak* or government postal system of roads and relay stations.

Despite its racially based caste system, the Sassanian Empire gave greater official recognition to the culture of its Semitic Aramaean subjects in what is now Iraq than did the Romans and Byzantines to their Semites in Syria. A very large Jewish population also flourished under Sassanian rule, with its own semi-autonomous "Exilarchate" leadership based in Iraq, a community that would flourish until the advent of modern Zionism. The position of the most powerful Semitic people, the Arabs, was different. At times they were allies, vassals or enemies of the Sassanians.

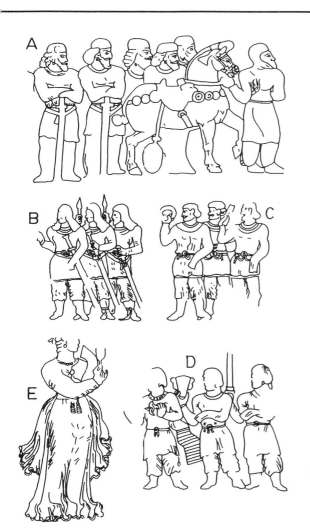

6. Sassanian infantry and dismounted horsemen.

A Attendants at an enthronement, late 3rd or early 4th centuries AD. A groom wearing what appears to be a headcloth or close-fitting hood leads the new ruler's horse. The "horns" at the front and rear of its saddle are clearly visible, as are decorated breast and breeching straps, a long pendant tassle from the rear of the saddle, a broad girth, knotted tail and a bridle with decorations attached. The standing figures behind this horse may be dismounted cavalry or members of the lesser aristocracy judging from their rather simple low-domed caps and long straight swords (in situ, Bishapur, Iran).

B Guards at the Triumph of Shapur I. Three men on the left are probably simple guardsmen with very long hair and no hats. They are armed with short spears and the normal long Sassanian sword. However, the scabbards are pulled up tightly so that the pommels touch the men's chests. This would suggest that they are equipped to serve, or at least to parade, on foot (in situ, Bishapur, Iran).

C & D Tribute-bearers at the Triumph of Shapur I. Beneath rows of aristocrats and warriors are a large number of tribute-bearers, of which these are a few. Some of their costumes and hairstyles differ from that of the Persian military elite and the objects they carry seem to symbolize the wealth of both the Empire's far-flung provinces and of neighbours who might have recognized Sassanian suzereinty. The last man on the right of D, for example, carries a sword and appears to wear a turban. At this period a turban would identify him as an Indian or as coming from what is now Afghanistan. Throughout the Sassanian and subsequent early Islamic periods India was famous for the quality of its true-steel sword blades (in situ, Bishapur, Iran).

E Rock-relief carving of a woman or goddess presenting a gift or victory symbol to a Sassanian ruler, late 3rd or early 4th century AD. Apart from her very long dress, this female figure's costume is similar to that of the male elite. Her jacket is identical except that it is secured by a single rather than a doubled clasp (in situ, Tang-i Qandil, Iran).

7. Facsimile of a wall-painting found in the synagogue at Dura Europos, Syria, original early-3rd century AD. This copy of a famous painting of the "Battle of Eben-Ezer" was based on notes and sketches made when the original had just been uncovered by archaeologists, before its colours and minor details began to fade. The figures shown here are all infantrymen; the few cavalrymen on the painting being completely unarmoured. They are taken from both sides in the Battle of Eben-Ezer - Israelites and Philistines - the artist indicating no distinction between the two. When the wall painting was made Dura Europos was a Roman frontier town, very close to the Sassanian border. It lay in the midst of a war-torn zone patrolled by Roman and Sassanian armies and by indigenous Arab tribes. Hence it is not surprising that the soldiers in the Battle of Eben-Ezer bear little relation to Romans. These wear mail hauberks, some with long sleeves, some with short, and three also have mail coifs over their heads. Such a reliance on mail suggests strong Sassanian influence. On the other hand their swords are relatively short like the Roman gladius or early Arab *sayf*. Their shields are made from reeds bound with strips of leather, a system that would continue to be used by Iraqi warriors for at least another six hundred years. Altogether these soldiers probably reflect Sassanian infantry forces from the largely Arab western parts of the Empire, rather than Roman frontier troops (Yale University Dept. of History, New Haven, USA).

Whatever their position, however, the Arabs could never be so easily controlled by the Sassanians as could the Aramaeans or Jews.

Most senior military positions were held by the Sassanian ruling family. The army itself was under the *Iran-Spahbad* commander-in-chief who also acted as Minister of War and as a chief peace negotiator. In the early days the actual war leader was called the *Arteshtaransalar*. Lesser *Spahbads* could command a field army while the regional *marzbans* and *kanarangs* could be regarded as field generals. Virtually nothing is known about the junior officer ranks though there was a group of *arzbad-i-aspwaraghan* "cavalry instructors" who toured the Empire, checking on the training and discipline of troops. Another vital and usually very experienced officer was the *Iran-anbaraghbad* responsible for equipment stored in *anbaragh* magazines in the *ganj* arsenals. Then there was the *stor-bezashk* senior vet who looked after the cavalry elite's mounts.

Troops made obeisance to their leaders at regular reviews and were presumably also inspected. In the early days great feudal barons served without pay and were expected to bring their own fully equiped

followers. A Sassanian legal code known as the "Book of a Thousand Legal Decisions" listed the horsemen expected from each parcel of land as well as those "free men" dependent upon and equipped by the local magnates. On the death of a cavalryman his land reverted to the state unless his heir wished to become a cavalry soldier, in which case his name was entered in the government's *Nipek* or "List of Horsemen".

Great magnates had their own full-time guard units, sometimes consisting of warrior-slaves, and such guardsmen may have fought as infantry while the freeborn warriors were cavalry. In the 4th century the Sassanian Emperor Shapur II, under military pressure from the Roman Empire, copied his enemies and raised an elite force of 1,000 professional cavalry. This versatile and powerful unit was forbidden to give quarter or to stop for booty. At the other end of the military scale were companies of infantry archers which, under their *tirbad* officers, were stationed in the villages. Other *paighan* infantry were commanded by *paighansalahs*. Sometimes paid, but often not. This infantry acted as a regional gendarmerie recruited from the local peasantry, having very low status and doubtful military reliability.

Strategy & Tactics

In many respects the tactics of the Sassanian army were similar to those of the Parthians. The main difference was that while horse-archers dominated Parthian forces, close combat cavalry armed with spear were tactically more important in Sassanian forces who also made greater use of infantry archers and gave a more prominent role to auxiliaries. In fact the addition of north Arabian light cavalry to the Persian heavy cavalry elite made a very effective force.

The sophisticated Sassanian state similarly made great use of embassies and spies, particularly in its relations with the Roman Empire. According to the later "Book of the Crown" members of a proposed Sassanian embassy were tested for loyalty by being sent on lesser missions within the Empire where their actions were recorded by a state security system.

The Sassanians were clearly capable of fielding more than one army, each following different routes and campaigning in widely separated regions. During the final brutal war against the Romano-Byzantines the Sassanians even attempted naval expeditions in the Mediterranean and though they were not particularly successful they did sieze the island of Rhodes in 625 AD. At the same time some wars

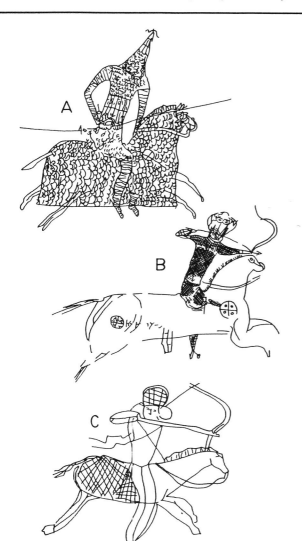

8. Graffiti from buildings and walls in Dura Europos, north-eastern Syria 3rd century AD.

A The most famous graffito from Dura Europos is this sketch of a heavily armoured Sassanian or late Parthian cavalryman. The warrior is equipped as what the Romans called a *clibanarius*, though kitted out in a Persian manner. The artist has exaggerated the point of his segmented helmet but has clearly shown a mail aventail covering the rider's face. The upper part of his chest and from his waist to knees are covered in mail, almost certainly one long mail hauberk. But around his waist the man also has a lamellar cuirass. The numerous lines across his arms and legs are more of a problem. They could indicate an Iranian horseman's typical baggy clothing or could show laminated armour for the limbs, as appears in the art of Transoxania a few centuries later. But there is little evidence that such laminated arm defences ever actually went above the elbows. The man's long spear is evident and the hilt of a sword or dagger is visible behind his back. The horse is protected by a large scale bard and the animal also seems to have a characterisic Iranian metal caveson bit around its entire nose (Yale University Art Gallery, New Haven, USA).

B Graffito showing an apparently unarmoured horse-archer. Such troops formed the bulk of both Parthian and early Sassanian cavalry. This lesser known sketch on a plaster wall may have been made by one of the Sassanian soldiers who took Dura Europos from the Romans in 252AD. Perhaps it is a self portrait (Yale University Art Gallery, New Haven, USA).

C Graffito from the "House of the Roman Scribes" again showing an unarmoured horse-archer with a very large hat or crown and full hair on both sides of his head. The horse appears to have a very large saddle blanket as there would be no reason for it to wear armour only over its rump (Yale University Art Gallery, New Haven, USA).

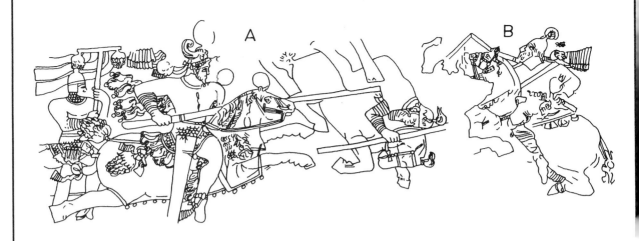

9. The Sassanian cavalry elite.

A Rock-relief carving of Hormizd II and his standard-bearer overthrowing a rebel, early 4th century AD. On the left the standard-bearer carried a T-shaped pole with three streamers and two large tassels. This is the best surviving illustration of a Sassanian imperial banner. The standard-bearer himself has a short jacket over a scale or more probably mail armour. Note that the folds of his long sleeves are indicated by parallel lines similar to those on the famous Dura Europos *clibanarius* graffito. There is also a mail or scale aventail or coif hanging from beneath his helmet which is in turn probably covered by a fabric cap. The man's quiver containing arrows with their points uppermost hangs from loose straps on his right hip. The King of Kings Hormizd II, at the centre of the picture, is equipped in the same manner - though more magnificently. He wields his thick lance with both hands, is bare-necked beneath an elaborate crown and wears a jacket which opens down his chest over a short mail or scale hauberk. The jacket is decorated with huge shoulder pompoms; another mark of rulership. Beneath its tassels and pompoms Hormizd's horse has a relatively short caparison or horse-armour, perhaps lined with felt or quilting as was the case by the 7th and 8th centuries AD. The identity of the horseman whom Hormizd overthrows is unknown, but he is clearly not a Roman. He is equipped in an essentially Persian manner and may represent a rebel (in situ, Naqsh-i Rustam, Iran).

B Rock-relief carving of an enemy overthrown by the army of Hormizd II, early 4th century AD. This figure has sometimes been identified as a defeated Roman and he is certainly different to the other horsemen in several respects. His helmet seems to incorporate a face-mask or visor, though a closer study of the original carving is needed to confirm this. Anthropomorphic visors were used by late Roman cavalry but this figure could equally represent another warrior from the Sassanian Empire's western frontier such as an Armenian or Georgian (in situ, Naqsh-i Rustam, Iran).

C Reconstruction of a Sassanian or vassal heavy cavalryman from the western regions of the Empire, based on the Naqsh-i Rustam rock-relief carvings.

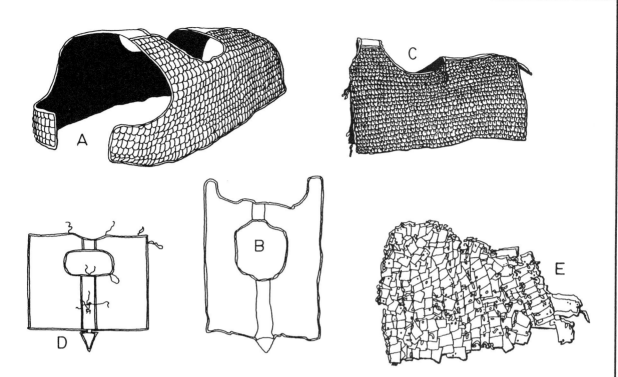

10. Horse-Armour. The most amazing military finds from Dura Europos were two virtually complete horse-armours. They are of an early form in which the animal's body, except for neck and head, were protected by a single sheet of barding. The neck would obviously have been protected by a separate crinet, one of which may also have been found in the ruins of Dura Europos.

A & B Iron scale horse-armour from Dura Europos, probably Parthian mid-3rd century AD. Both the Dura Europos horse-armours consisted of metal scales attached to a linen lining. They both had simple holes for the saddle, exposed panels of cloth without scales along the spine in front and behind the saddle, and small triangular flaps of armour to protect the base of the horse's tail. The only significant difference was that this iron scale armour included two flap-like extensions which wrapped around the front of the animal's chest. The lacing system which secured this armour around the horse also appears to be missing (Higgins Armory, Worcester, USA).

C & D Bronze scale horse-armour from Dura Europos, probably Parthian mid-3rd century AD. In the second barding from Dura Europos the scales are approximately 3.5 x 2.5 cms in size and are stapled to each other as well as being fastened to a linen base. Most of the laces which fastened the armour across the horse's chest survive, as do several other sets of laces around the saddle-hole and on the unprotected panel behind the saddle. Some of these may have secured the armour to the saddle itself but others almost certainly carried archery equipment. The fact that the top of the horses back is virtually unprotected points to the fact that the main threat came from archery rather than a blow with a sword or comparable weapon. Nevertheless the horse probably had some kind of quilted or padded protection over these areas, as suggested on the later rock-cut equestrian statue at Taq-i Bustan (National Museum, Damascus, Syria).

E Hardened-leather probable crinet of a horse-armour from Dura Europos, probably Parthian mid-3rd century AD. The precise identification of this triangular sheet of leather lamellar armour remains a matter of debate. It was, however, most likely one half of a crinet to protect a horse's neck. The hardened leather lamellae are not lacquered, unlike many of those found in Central Asia, but seem to have been painted or stained red. Most are approximately 7 x 4-5 cms in size, though a row of larger lamellae at one end are approximately 9 x 7 cms. The top and two sides of the sheet, as shown in this view, also have a broad strip of more flexible leather forming an edge. Quite what really was the top, however, remains unclear (Yale University Art Gallery, New Haven, USA).

11.   Metalwork & Jewelry.

A   Carved intaglio gemstone, Sassanian 4th century AD. This tiny carving is believed to show Shapur I capturing the Roman Emperor Valerian in 260 AD. The Roman is portrayed with remarkable accuracy and so one can assume that the Persian is similarly accurate. Most of his costume, as well as the ceremonial paraphernalia of his horse harness, mirror those seen in earlier rock-relief carvings. Here, however, the Sassanian's sword is slightly shorter and his great beard, instead of being tied into a tuft, is pushed inside a broadened chin-strap (Bibliotheque Nationale, Paris, France).

B   Detail from a silver dish, Sassanian 4th century AD. The Sassanians used a more sophisticated form of fencing grip than that seen in the Roman World. It was later adopted by the Muslim Arabs who in turn took it to Spain. The style, which permitted a thrust and a more controlled swing, eventually spread throughout Europe where it was known as the "Italian grip" (British Museum, London, England).

C   Silver plate, Sassanian 4th or 5th centuries AD. Here the hero Tahmagdast "Mighty Hand" hunts wild beasts from camel-back while a smaller figure, probably a slave girl, rides behind him carrying his quiver. This motif remained popular in subsequent Islamic art where the subject was changed into Varahran (Bahran Gur) the "Mighty Hunter" attended by a paramour playing a musical instrument. Even as late as the First World War elite Arab tribal warriors often had a servant riding behind their camel saddle carrying their rifle (Metropolitan Museum of Art, New York, USA).

D   Silver dish, Sassanian late 4th century AD. Here a Persian ruler believed to represent Shapur II makes an archetypal "Parthian Shot" over the rump of his horse. Such a tactic could cause havoc among unexpecting Roman troops. It was not, of course, a Persian invention having been developed amongst the nomad horse archers of the Central Asian steppes and would remain in use by such peoples even after they adopted firearms. This silver plate is also interesting because it includes a very early representation of a curved or angled sabre-hilt on an otherwise straight sword (State Hermitage Museum, St. Petersburg, Russia).

11. (cont.)

E   Silver dish, Sassanian 4th century AD. Another illustration of Shapur II shows a mixture of old-fashioned and more modern equipment. A long and apparently empty tube-like quiver hangs from narrow straps which go beneath a lower belt, probably for the sword whose hilt is visible behind the rider's seat. More modern is a completely new form of saddle reflecting Central Asian and even Chinese influence. There are no longer any "horns"; instead a low saddle-bow or pommel without a comparable cantle at the rear. This would seem strange to a modern rider but saddles with high pommels and no visible cantles clearly appear elsewhere in late Sassanian and early Byzantine art (Freer Gallery of Art, Washington, USA).

F   Silver dish, Sassanian 5th century AD. This detail from a slightly later dish again shows what would eventually be called the "Italian grip". The sword is being wielded during a lion hunt (British Museum, London, England).

G   Silver plate, Sassanian 4th century AD. A detail of Shapur II's right hand pulling a bow-string in a variation of the "Persian-draw" where the two middle fingers lock over the thumb which actually holds the string (State Hermitage Museum, St. Petersburg, Russia).

H   Silver plate, Sassanian 5th century AD. Detail of an archer's hand pulling a bow-string in another variation of the "Persian-draw". Here crossed straps held a protective leather flap inside of the fingers (Metropolitan Museum of Art, New York, USA).

I   Silver plate, Sassanian probably 4th century AD. Detail of Ardashir's right hand pulling a bow-string in a further variation of the "Persian-draw". A protective leather flap is again being used (Archaeological Museum, Tehran, Iran).

J   Silver plate, Sassanian late 5th century AD. Detail of the Sassanian ruler Peroz's right hand pulling a bow-string with the classic Central Asian "Mongol thumb-draw". This would remain the chief method of drawing a bow, particularly in war, throughout the Middle East and most of Asia though weaker earlier methods continued to be used to avoid fatigue (State Hermitage Museum, St. Petersburg, Russia).

between Rome and the Sassanians were very vicious and both sides destroyed enemy cities and massacred their populations .

On land, battles could last for several days. Before they began, Zoroastrian mobad priests would consecrate a near by spring with holy water and a ram would be sacrificed. The enemy would be called upon to submit to the Sassanian King of Kings and accept Zoroastrianism. If they refused, an arrow or simply a stick representing an ancient arrow would be shot as a sign that battle had begun. Commanders exhorted their men with promises of rewards in this world and the next and condemned the "unbelieving"

enemy. The battle itself normally started with cries of Mard u mard, "Man to Man", provoking the enemy into combat with Sassanian champions. If the King of Kings was present his throne was erected on a hill or would at least be put in the centre of the army surrounded by four flags. Within these stood the ruler's servants and guards, while beyond them were ranged archers and infantry. Sometimes the ruler's harem or household would also accompany the army. If the ruler was not himself present, the Commander in Chief would similarly sit enthroned.

Trumpets signalled an attack and maintained the soldiers' morale; drums also being characteristic of the eastern regions where an army's drum-master was so important to battlefield control that his death could cause an entire army to flee. By the 6th century Sassanian archers normally advanced in serried ranks, shooting volleys at command. Sassanian forces also made infantry charges. Theoretically the centre of an army would be placed on high ground with the cavalry ahead and archers to their left. In one well recorded but disastrous battle against Ephthalite White Hun invaders in the 5th century the Sassanian army was drawn up in three divisions forming a single line eight rows deep. Such a static formation had little in common with the traditional "Battle Plan of the King of Kings" as recorded in the 13th century Persian Adab al Harb (Art of War) but is similar to the "Battle Plan of the Indians as invented by Garshasp (ancestor of the epic Persian hero Rustam)" in the same book. Perhaps this was the early Sassanian battle plan whereas the "Battle Plan of the King of Kings" reflected new Sassanian tactics adopted after a series of defeats by the Huns. The Sassanians did not apparently use the five-part Khamis battle plan employed by the early Muslim Arabs as this was essentially a Semitic concept reserved for the Middle Eastern armies. Nor was Sassanian military theory, as preserved in Islamic writings, based on Greek or Roman ideas though it did incorporate Greek technical terms. The Sassanians had their own effective way of assessing casualties. Before a campaign or battle every soldier put an arrow into a pannier. After the battle the survivors took one arrow back, those remaining representing the army's losses. Meanwhile the Sassanians normally took prisoners for sale as slaves or to colonize distant parts of their empire.

12. Horse Harness. Even highly stylized three-dimensional objects can often provide more accurate information than two-dimensional art.

A Silver horse's head, Sassanian 4th century AD. This head, with its detailed bridle and bit, perhaps formed part of a vessel or container. The bridle straps have a decorative surface with additional decoration on the cheek-straps and linkage. The broadened noseband is particularly interesting, perhaps being of plaited leather and recalling the bridles of the medieval Middle East. In fact, several aspects of this object suggest that it might be some centuries later than its supposed date (Louvre Museum, Paris, France).

B & C Gilded silver rhyton, Sassanian, perhaps 3rd or 4th centuries AD. This magnificent object, though broken in half and reassembled, may have been suspended from a larger structure as it apparently had a chain attached to the saddle. Among the most significant features are a frame-like metallic caveson bit which goes around and down the front of the animal's mouth. There is also a large tassle attached to the forelock and very large decorated medallions above each foreleg where the breast-strap divides before being attached to the saddle. The rectangular saddle-covering is distorted where the object was divided. But two of the four "horns" are clearly visible - though much less prominent than they would have been in reality (Severance Fund, Museum of Art, Cleveland, USA).

D Reconstruction of a saddled horse based on the gilded silver rhyton in the Cleveland Museum of Art.

Heavily armoured close-combat cavalry formed the core of a Sassanian army and were supported by light cavalry including horse-archers who were also useful for screening, skirmishing and harrassing the enemy. Generally speaking the light horse outnumbered armoured men by ten to one, as they had in Parthian times. Heavy cavalry could rarely break infantry with a direct charge and their primary role was to pin down enemy foot soldiers while the light cavalry worked around the enemy's flanks. To be effective the heavy horsemen had to manoeuvre in close-packed squadrons with the best protected troops at the front. The Sassanians' enemies needed heavy cavalry to face these Iranian *aswanan* and at first the Romans equipped such troops with captured Sassanian equipment.

The Sassanians did not use stirrups until the last few years of their empire. This reduced the number of shots available to a horse-archer but had much less impact on the effectiveness of spear-armed cavalry after the development of wood-framed saddles. Such horsemen could not use their spears in the couched manner, locked beneath their right arms as done by medieval western European knights, and instead used the two-handed technique shown in post

Hellenistic art. Here the weapon was usually thrust along the right side of the horse's head. The main problem lay in retrieving a weapon from a fallen foe and if a spear was laid across the horse's neck down the left side of its head such retrieval was virtually impossible.

The armour worn by Iranian elite cavalry was probably a response to the threat from archery, and the same was true of horse-armour since arrows could easily panic horses and break up cavalry formations. On the debit side heat loss was a problem for the relatively heavy-boned Persian horses which were less able to regulate body temperature than light-boned horses. Heavy cavalry horses also needed greater training and greater maturity to cope with the stress of carrying such weight. Not surprisingly the Romans considered the Sassanian armoured cavalry elite as brave but lacking in endurance.

Being virtually immune to arrows, Sassanian heavy cavalry could only be brought down with close-combat weapons such as the large lances they themselves used, while in a melee shorter weapons like swords would have been more practical. Shields were rarely carried by spear-armed cavalry before the advent of stirrups, though they are shown with swords. The later Sassanians also used a fencing style later known as the "Italian Grip" where the forefinger was wrapped around the quillons. This moved the centre of gravity closer to the point of a sword, permitting a harder blow and, more importantly, a forward lunge.

Meanwhile the bulk of Sassanian archers were now infantry who shot fast and accurately from behind wattle mantlets as the ancient Assyrians had done. Other Sassanian foot soldiers armed with spear and sword were also capable of meeting the Romans hand-to-hand. Roman tactics changed over the centuries but the essentials of Sassanian warfare did not. To some extent this reflected deep-seated conservatism, yet traditional Sassanian warfare remained highly effective and the Sassanian armoured cavalry elite was the prototype of the medieval European heavy cavalry knight.

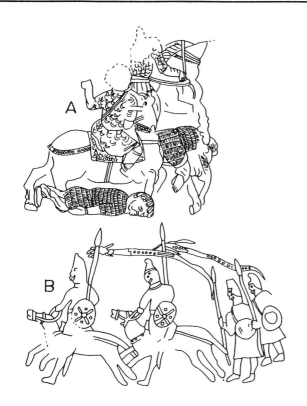

13.   Persian soldiers in Egyptian art.

A   "Siege of the Citadel of Faith", Coptic wood carving, 5th or 6th centuries AD. These figures come from a group of horsemen galloping around a castle defended by soldiers equipped in early Byzantine style. They represent the enemies of Christendom and are probably based on Sassanian troops. The upper two cavalrymen appear to be protected by scale armour; perhaps a Coptic artist's attempt to indicate lamellar. The lower two, one slumped forward over his saddle and the other fallen to the ground, wear mail hauberks. These two mailed men also have loose-fitting trousers and one rides with bare feet. Yet the position of the upright horseman's leg suggests the use of stirrups. This, plus several other details, could indicate that it was made a century or so later - perhaps in the very early Islamic period (ex-Staatliche Museen, Berlin, Germany; lost or destroyed during the Second World War).

B   "Pharoah's Army crossing the Red Sea", wall painting, Coptic 4th or 5th centuries AD. Crude and stylized enough to be regarded as folk-art, this painting shows cavalry and infantry equipped in an un-Roman manner. It may reflect the nearest important enemy - namely the Sassanian Empire or its regional allies. Both horsemen have long pennons on their lances which could be based on the windsock "dragon banners" used by several Middle Eastern armies. At least two figures have the forward-curled Phrygian caps popularly associated with Persians and all, whether on foot or horseback, carry a small round or oval shield in addition to a spear (in situ, Chapel of the Flight, Al Bagawat, Kharga Oasis, Egypt).

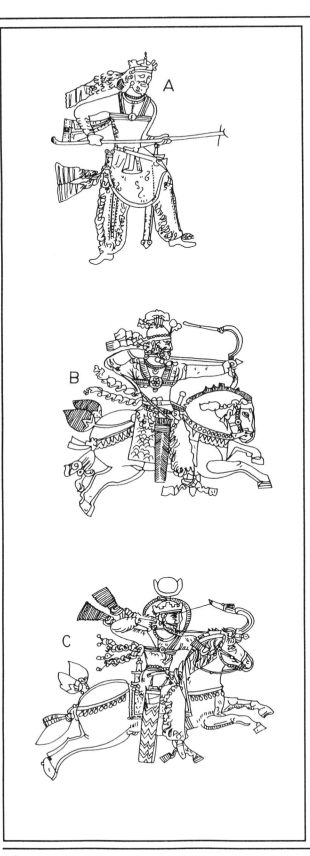

Medieval Islamic tradition believed that Persian archery declined from the reigns of Shapur I to that of the Varahran V "The Mighty Hunter" in the mid-5th century. Modern scholarship places this decline between 200 and 350 AD, though a theory that this period also saw the technology of armour becoming superior to bow technology is probably incorrect. In reality the Sassanian era saw a reversal to earlier traditions of Middle Eastern infantry archery, away from the Central Asian horse-archery tactics of the Parthians. This infantry archery tradition also influenced the Romans until Hun and later Avar invasions led to a new form of Romano-Byzantine cavalry. Infantry archery would also dominate Middle Eastern warfare until the end of the Umayyad Caliphate in the mid-8th century when Central Asian horse-archery finally took over.

Early Sassanian bows, whether used on foot or horseback, were similar to those of the Parthians and Scythians. Those of the later Sassanian period were virtually identical to those of the Huns and

15. Hunting.

A Fragment of a bronze statuette, Sassanian late 3rd or early 4th centuries AD. This figure is believed to represent the Sassanian Emperor Narseh using a javelin, a weapon that would remain popular in the Middle East for cavalry and infantry many centuries after it had been abandoned in Western Europe. In Sassanian sources it is normally only used for hunting. The head of the javelin appears to be barbed, though this might indicate the socket of its iron head (Islamische Museum, Staatliche Museen, Berlin, Germany).

B - D Silver repoussé bowl, Sassanian 5th century AD. The huntsmen armed with spears, bows and at least one sword on this silver bowl are dressed in more ordinary costume than appears in most Sassanian art. Two have their hair tied back with bandanas. They wear knee-length shirts or tunics and loose-fitting trousers. There is still no evidence of large Central Asian style riding boots. Each horseman also has what looks like a long cloth or scarf around his shoulders, a fashion which reappeared in the 13th century Middle East, being worn by a military elite. Perhaps it had never been abandoned. It is interesting to note that the saddles, apparently of the new form with raised saddle-bows or pommels, are secured by relatively simple knotted breeching straps but lack breast straps. No straps seem to attach bowcase and scabbard to a rider's waist-belt, but it seems unlikely that these weapons would still be hung from saddles at such a late date (State Hermitage Museum, St. Petersburg, Russia).

E Reconstruction of a Sassanian huntsman based on the silver repoussé bowl in the Hermitage.

Magyar Hungarians with a set-back grip, relatively short curved working parts, angled knees and long stiff ears. The upper limb of the bow was often longer than the lower. There is still argument about whether the Sassanians used the Turco-Mongol "thumb-draw". The Parthians probably did so, and at least one archer's thumb-ring was found in the ruins of mid-3rd century AD Dura Europos. The shape of arrows found at Dura Europos shows they could not have been shot using the Roman "Mediterranean draw", but whether they could have been loosed using the so-called "Persian draw" remains unclear. According to early Byzantine sources this was what Sassanians archers normally used. Here the lower three or middle two fingers held the bowstring, possibly locked by the thumb, while the index finger lay along the arrow. Such a style continued to be used in much of eastern Europe until the late Middle Ages. Available evidence suggests that the Sassanian Persians were actually among the last Middle Eastern archers to adopt the powerful Central Asian "thumb-draw"; after the Byzantines and even after the Arabs.

Powerful as Sassanian bows were, they were smaller than those of the Nubians as recorded in documents dealing with a failed Sassanian invasion of northern Sudan in the early 7th century. Nubian and Sudanese bows were of all-wood construction, being much the same as the traditional bows of pre- and early Islamic Arabia. The classic clash of Sassanian and Arabian archery techniques came at the decisive battle of Qadisiyah where Arab infantry archers shot heavy arrows which the Persians at first mocked as "spindles". But as a Sassanian survivor later stated: "These spindles continued to shower upon us until we were overwhelmed. Our archer would send an arrow from his *nawak* bow but it would merely attach itself to an Arab's clothes whereas their arrows would rend the mail hauberk and the cuirass we had on". Arab sources confirm that the Sassanians used *nawak* arrows but said that they, in turn, were able to penetrate strong armour. The *nawak* was an interesting device almost certainly invented by the Sassanians for use against nomadic Turkish invaders. It consisted of a grooved channel or "arrow-guide" held against the bow to form a temporary crossbow. Short darts, from 10 to 40 cms long, were shot down this "arrow-guide" and had great penetration at close range. More importantly they had greater range than normal arrows, were virtually invisible in flight, could be carried in large numbers by light troops and could not be shot back by an enemy unless he also used a *nawak*. Meanwhile arrow-guides were not recorded in Central Asia or China,though they were used by Korean infantry far to the east.

One other feature which caught the attention of the Sassanians' western foes was their use of war elephants, which the Parthians had rarely done. These were brought from India, perhaps via the Sassanian Empire's close contacts with the Kushans. Some carried several men in wooden towers and were said to have been used as a living "wall" behind the army. Other evidence suggests that Sassanian war elephants were placed behind the cavalry but ahead of the infantry. On one occasion in the late 4th century Sassanian archers kept the Romans' heads down while the elephants advanced to attack but at other times Sassanian war elephants were less successful, the Romano-Byzantines capturing twenty-four at Malatya in 575 AD. Other elephants were taken when the Romano-Byzantines invaded Sassanian-ruled Iraq and perhaps for this reason very few are mentioned during the Muslim Arab invasion in the 7th century.

16. Late Sassanian Animal Harness.

A Bronze statuette, Sassanian late 6th or early 7th centuries AD. This little horseman is believed to represent Khusru II. He appears to wear a gaiter around his lower leg above the shoe. This feature had not been seen earlier but would become characteristic of early medieval Islamic as well as Byzantine horsemen and was probably of Avar origin. As such it reflects a new wave of Central Asian military and riding influences seen in Iran during the final Sassanian century. Other important features concerning the horse harness are a crudely represented curved curb bit and a pronounced pommel or saddle-bow in front of the rider (State Hermitage Museum, St. Petersburg, Russia).

B Silver rhyton in the form of a horse's head, Sassanian 6th or 7th centuries AD. Like several items of late Sassanian art, this object may in fact be "post-Sassanian"; in other words from early Islamic Persia. The bridle and bit are typical of both periods. The bridle itself is a decorated but structurally simple system. The bit is, however, of an old-fashioned snaffle type with large rectangular psalion cheek pieces. The looped ribbon fluttering from the cheek linkage was a popular form of Sassanian harness decoration which did not survive long into the Islamic period (Art Museum, Cincinnati, USA).

C Stucco plaque from Tarkhan Eshqabad, Sassanian or early Islamic Iran, late 6th or 7th centuries AD. Once again it is impossible to give a precise date to these fragments of plaster decoration. But it is equally clear that the first phase of the Muslim conquest of Iran had little effect on the military equipment or horse-harness of the area. Here a hunter on horseback strikes down at a missing animal, still using the two-handed lance technique. He has no stirrups but the bridle includes a curb bit and the breeching straps seem to be divided into two just behind the saddle or saddle-blanket. The decorative ribbons around the animal's legs were another fashion which survived for a further thousand years (Museum of Fine Arts, Boston, USA).

D Stucco plaque from Tarkhan Eshqabad, Sassanian or early Islamic Iran, late 6th or 7th centuries AD. Another fragment of plaster decoration poses the same problems. The fact that it probably shows Bahram Gur "The Great Hunter" riding a camel and not a horse does not mean that it came from the Arab-Islamic rather than Sassanian period. One feature, though, is potentially very important. This rider seems to be using a stirrup as indicated not only by a line around his foot and the apparent stirrup leather above, but also by the angle of the foot itself. Early Arab sources clearly state that the first Muslims did not use stirrups until they adopted them in north-eastern Iran or Turkestan in the late 7th century. What is less well known is that these same sources state that stirrups had been known for at least half a century earlier, but were regarded by the Arabs as a Persian device for men too feeble to leap upon their horses. At the same time these early Arabs may have used some form of stirrup when mounting or riding camels (Museum of Fine Arts, Boston, USA).

E & F Silver plate, Sassanian late 6th or early 7th centuries AD. These two details from a plate believed to portray the late Sassanian ruler Khusru II have been included because one has the clearest representation of a large saddle-bow or pommel in front of the rider's hips. Once again there is no indication of a comparable cantle at the back. Other interesting details include a sword hilt behind the man's buttocks. Swords in this position appear in several Sassanian sources and show that such large straight swords were hung vertically or even with their hilts leaning slightly to the rear. A little later they would be supported in a different manner with the grip leaning forward, as was already the case among Central Asian warriors. The quiver hanging vertically on the man's right hip is held by two straps tied to a low-slung narrow belt. A large dagger of Central Asian or Transoxanian design is slung horizontally across the right hip with its grip to the rear. This weapon's sheath goes beneath the archery belt while its grip seems to be tucked beneath the slanting sword-belt. Such an impractical, uncomfortable and damaging method must surely be an artist's error. This form of dagger was a new phenomenon in Sassanian art. In their Transoxanian homeland such weapons were slung horizontontally across the front of the belly or slightly to the left, not on the right as here. A second detail of the horse's head shows several traditional features including a trimmed mane with an upstanding tuft on the upper part of the neck, a ribbon attached to the cheek linkage, a plume between the horse's ears, a doubled neck collar, the probable buckle for doubled-cheek straps, and a prominent curved curb bit attached to a rigid metalic caveson around the animal's nose. The seemingly archaic caveson was still being used in 7th and 8th century Transoxania to the north-east and would appear in highly stylized form in early Islamic art for many more years (Bibliotheque Nationale, Paris, France).

Royal Troops

Most Sassanian rulers took an active part in warfare while the *Vuzurg-Framadar* "Grand Vizier" was always deeply involved in military affairs. The second highest rank at Court was the Emperor's Sword Bearer who, unlike most other officials, wore military costume during ceremonies. He carried the ruler's sword in a gold scabbard, and a belt decorated with gemstones and pearls. Next came the *Spahbad* army chiefs, *Padgospan* lesser military leaders and *Marzban* provincial military governors. Other military officials at Court were the Commander of the Royal Bodyguards, the Head of the Palace Security Service and Prison, the Palace Doorkeeper, the Head of the Royal Arsenal and the Chief Palace Supplies Officer. There were also a number of privileged *azatan* "free warriors" at Court, perhaps being the military instructors who trained young princes.

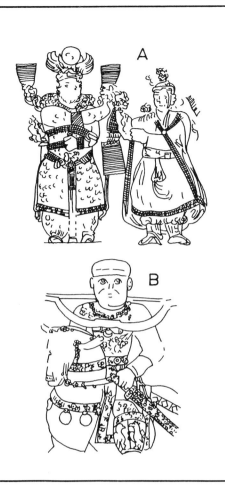

17. Rock relief-carvings, Sassanian early 7th century AD; the late-Sassanian elite.

A One of the last Sassanian rulers, Khosru II, offers or accepts a symbolic gift to or from a senior military leader, ally or divine figure. Sassanian art was still as hierarchical as it had always been and its main function remained royal propaganda. By remaining rigidly within long-established Iranian styles it also proclaimed the Sassanians as the legitimate successors of ancient Persian Emperors. Here both figures wear long kaftan tunics and very baggy trousers. The figure on the right, presumably a military figure, also seems to have short riding boots or gaiters and clearly wears the voluminous cloak that became a mark of the military aristocracy in Byzantium as well as Iran (in situ, Taq-i Bustan, Iran).

B Among several detailed representations of huntsmen on the low-relief carvings which surround the famous Taq-i Bustan grotto is a relatively undamaged portrayal of a horseman carrying his powerful composite bow around his neck. This appears to have been common practice among Persians and Byzantines as well as subsequent early Islamic warriors who, unlike Turco-Mongol warriors, did not always use bowcases. On his head is a low form of plain *qalansuwa* cap. His tight-fitting tunic and baggy trousers are highly decorated, as are his saddle and harness. He wears a thickly padded gaiter around his lower leg while his straight sword is now slung at an angle from two straps to a waist-belt as a clear indication of Transoxanian or Central Asian influence upon very late Sassanian military equipment. The horse's head is damaged but almost certainly includes a fully developed curb bit (in situ, Taq-i Bustan, Iran).

The Sassanian King of Kings had more than one guard unit, the most important apparently being the *Pushtighbansalar*. The *Varhranighan-khvadhay* "Thousand Immortals" were based on the famous Achaemenid guard unit of the same name. A third elite were the *Jan-avaspar* "those who sacrifice themselves" though this was not necessarily a guards regiment. It may have consisted of mercenaries, one of their leaders apparently being a Greek. Cavalry stationed at Court formed a social as well as military elite, enjoying "the warmth of the ruler's sunlight", but most Sassanian cavalry lived on their own estates.

A sophisticated Empire with ancient traditions naturally had a highly developed system of banners. Two main types were used; a long narrow banderole and a rectangular panel hanging from a crossbar. The banderole was used by small units called *Vasht*. Larger units or *Drafsh* may have used the crossbar type as, presumably, did Gund armies. The most important Sassanian flag was the *Drafsh-i-Kavyan*, a huge banner with a legendary history. It was carried by five *mobad* priests ahead of the army and, as the symbol of Sassanian legitimacy, its loss to the Muslim Arabs had immense repercussions. According to legend this *Drafsh-i-Kavyan* was made by the magical smith, Kave, in ancient times and was used by the Aryans when they rose against their mythical Semitic oppressor Dahak. The version captured by the Arabs in 635 AD was a leather sheet seven metres long and five wide, decorated with yellow, red and violet embroidery, gems and pearls, topped by a golden ball and with red, yellow and violet streamers.

Colour symbolism was important to the Sassanians, as it was to their Central Asian Turkish rivals. But whereas the Turks used colours to represent the four points of the compass, Sassanian ymbolism may have reflected the Indian origins of he game of chess where yellow and green teams allied gainst red and black. Yellow and green appear as ignificant colours for Sassanian kings in Persian art nd the Sassanian concern with symbolic colours is choed in the later Persian Shahnamah epic which ecounts the deeds of ancient Persian heroes. This reoccupation was inherited by some Muslim military lites who then transmitted it to Europe where it may ave provided the foundation for medieval heraldry.

Other objects associated with the greatest of assanian rulers were kept in a sort of reliquary, many eing captured by the Muslims on the fall of the mpire. They included the crown, tunic, armour and word of Khusru II, the captured crown reportedly eing hung in the Kaaba at Mecca, the most important f Islamic shrines. The scale pattern on surviving te Sassanian weapons and helmets is believed to epresent the feathers of the Simurgh or Varanga, a ythical bird with protective powers. This decoration as copied by the Huns who took it to Europe where is found on 6th and 7th century weaponry. More nportant was the elaborate doubled belt with corative pendants worn as a mark of rank by later assanian warriors. It had Turkish origins but ontinued to be used by the Muslim Arab and Persian ccessors of the Sassanians as late as the Crusader eriod. Various forms of headgear similarly indicated atus or honour. The basic Persian cap evolved from e nomad's *bashliq*. Those worn by Sassanian rulers d jewelled diadems; those of the military elite being corated with pearls and streamers as shown in late assanian and early Islamic Persian art.

Basically, Iranian costume changed little over ousands of years, consisting of a long sleeved loose-tting coat opening down the front, long trousers, latively tight boots and a cap. Such clothes were signed for a horseman. Some of these items, most viously the cap, were decorated with motifs which ight have indicated a particular guards regiment. thers might have had ancient clan or tribal origins ke the tamgas of Central Asia. Many were abstract t there were also eagles, dragons, sun and moon. mail hauberk found on the corpse of a Sassanian lled in a mine beneath Dura Europos appeared to e decorated with a trident motif in bronze mail links.

Gilded or polished bronze equipment was still being used at the end of the Sassanian Empire, for example senior generals defeated by the Byzantines in 625 and 627 having a gilded cuirass and a gilded sword. A fragment of late Sassanian or very early Islamic lamellar armour excavated at Kasr-i Abu Nasr consisted of iron and bronze elements. Although lamellar made something of a comeback near the end of the Sassanian era, it was a steppe nomadic form of armour more associated with the Parthians. On the other hand the famous description by Heliodorus of a fully armoured 3rd century Iranian heavy cavalryman states that he was almost completely encased in bronze or iron, with a one-piece masked helmet covering his head except for the eyes, his body from shoulders to knees covered with a suit of small overlapping bronze or iron plates, and with greaves for legs and feet. His horse was similarly protected; its head with a metal plate, its back and flanks by a blanket of thin iron plates while its legs also had some form of greaves.

Archaeological evidence from the early Parthian period suggests that such heavy armour was worn over separate leather, linen or felt padding. In the climate of the Middle East this would have been horribly hot, which was why lamellar, though often introduced by Asiatic invaders, was gradually abandoned each time in favour of less effective but cooler mail armour. The mail hauberk worn by the Sassanian slain beneath Dura Europos had short sleeves and reached just below the groin. Other Sassanian mail, particularly in the 6th century, was longer with full-length sleeves. It is even possible that Sassanian influence spread as far as barbarian Germany and that the Germanic name for a mail hauberk, *serk*, came from the Persian *zirrh*.

Certainly the Muslim Arab conquerors were impressed by the volume of equipment they captured, particularly in the eastern Sassanian and Transoxanian military bases which the Arabs called "The Forges of Sughd". Much evidence exists to suggest that the Sassanians were in advance of the Romans and Byzantines in military metallurgy and that the technique of casting rather than forging sword-blades had reached Iran from India and China by the 3rd century AD. Like the early Indian sword, fully developed Sassanian swords were very long, often as long as 1.2 metres including the hilt. Even the early Sassanian sword found beneath Dura Europos had a 64.5 cms blade plus a 14.5 cms tang. Such heavy weapons were carried in scabbards with long "scabbard-slides" for the belt. This device spread the weight along a fragile leather and wood scabbard. It appeared in 5th century BC China where it was associated with an early development of cavalry warfare but may actually have been invented by Iranian-speaking nomads related to those Kushans who established a state in Central Asia and northern India in the first centuries AD.

According to 4th century Armenian sources, the Sassanians wore a long sword on their left hip, a short sword on the right. A warrior would first put on a loose garment, then a first belt. Next a sword-belt to which both short and long swords were attached; after that trousers, leggings and finally a small dagger which was obscured by the "pleats" of his baggy trousers. By the late 6th century Sassanian contacts with Central Asian invaders led to minor changes to scabbards as well as to armour and archery. Swords came to be hung by straps from two attachment points on the same side of a scabbard rather than the old scabbard-slide, a system that was probably better for a horseman and clearly more convenient for a man on foot.

The Sassanians, like the Romans, rode full-sized horses, not small Asiatic ponies. The main riding horse of the early medieval Middle East probably looked like a large Arabian, though as yet the true Arabian breed was just being "created" in Arabia itself. Meanwhile in Transoxania another of the great horse breeds of the world, the Akel Tepe, was also emerging. The basic Sassanian cavalry mount was, however, the Nicaean breed raised in the Median steppes of western Iran. Other important horse-raising areas wholly or partially controlled by the Sassanians were the Jazira (Mesopotamia) of northern Iraq and the Mughan steppes of Azarbayjan. But rich as these regions were, they could not produce the vaste horse herds raised by Central Asian nomads. Hence the Persians, like the Arabs, aimed at quality rather than quantity. For the Iranians this meant size and as cavalry horses grew bigger so new bridle controls had to be developed. This in turn led to a separation

18. Rock relief-carvings, Sassanian early 7th century AD; a late Sassanian imperial hunt.

A A hunting scene at Taq-i Bustan takes place in marshes around the head of the Arabian Gulf. Here a gigantic figure of the King of Kings towers over attendants who include two boatmen and at least one court lady playing a harp. A full band of harpists occupy a second boat. The oversized ruler draws a massive bow using a form of thumb-draw. The hilt of a sword slung at an acute angle is visible on his left hip while a dagger hangs vertically on his right hip (in situ, Taq-i Bustan, Iran).

B One of several horse-archers chases wild animals. Like the more elaborately carved horseman with a bow around his neck, this man wears a low cap, knee-length tunic with tight sleeves and has his straight sword hung at an angle. The horse clearly has a curb bit and there appears to be a raised cantle at the rear of the saddle. Unfortunately the damaged condition of the rider's foot makes it impossible to state with certainty whether he rides with a stirrup though on balance it appears that he might (in situ, Taq-i Bustan, Iran).

C A line of somewhat damaged camels depicted carrying slaughtered animals from the scene of the Imperial Hunt. Their harness seems to be exactly the same as the portrayed in earlier and later sources from Syria and Iraq (in situ, Taq-i Bustan, Iran).

D Elephants played an important role in Sassanian armies, particularly in the final century. These elephants are taking part in a hunt rather than a battle but their harness is likely to have been the same. Each animal carries two men who occupy positions comparable to those in the art of Mughul India a thousand years later. A sequence of blanket-like sheets over the elephants' backs are also similar to those seen in India but are very different to those illustrated in the art of medieval Indo-China. Of particular interest is the way in which two riders on the lower left-hand elephant secure themselves. The man at the back has his leg through a rope running beneath the animal's tail while the man in front tucks his foot beneath one of the ropes running beneath the animal's belly. This is identical to the system in medieval and later India. It would probably also have been used by the Abyssinian invaders of southern Arabia (in situ, Taq-i Bustan, Iran).

E Reconstruction of a late Sassanian war elephant based on rock-relief carvings at Taq-i Bustan.

A

B

C

D

E

between Asiatic and "Classical" (Middle Eastern and European) riding techniques, the latter evolving from the Persian style. Unlike the Greeks and Arabs, the Iranians no longer leapt into the saddles of their taller horses but were helped to mount "in the Persian fashion". But this still did not involve stirrups. It appears that the first Sassanians had a framed saddle of the "horned" variety also used by the Romans. Around the 4th century this was replaced by a framed saddle with a pommel or saddle-bow, a change which remains something of a mystery as the saddle-bow would seem to have given less stability than the "horned" saddle. On the other hand the "horned" saddle was never used in Central Asia and would have been unsuitable for a horse-archer. So perhaps the Sassanian adoption of the saddle-bow type, as also used by the Huns, reflected a revival of horse-archery around the same time. The latter saddle was also introduced to the Roman Army by Constantine in the early 4th century, their weight being specified by the Roman Emperor Theodosius a century later.

Stirrups could be used without a saddle frame and although most historians have explained their development in military terms, one of the most immediate effects of using a stirrup is to reduce tiredness and cold legs resulting from impaired circulation. True stirrups had first appeared in one of the coldest parts of the world - Central Asia and northern China - by the 4th century AD, but why the primitive leather loop or "toe-stirrup" was known in northern India three hundred years earlier remains a mystery. Whether this Indian "toe-stirrup" had any influence upon Sassanian Iran is also unknown, though it clearly appears in Egyptian art of the 6th or 7th centuries and continued to be used in the Sudan until modern times.

Horse-armour changed during the Sassanian period. In the 3rd century most was of felt with the best being of iron or bronze scales, perhaps with leather lamellar for the animal's neck. Most Sassanian and early Islamic horse-armour continued to be of leather or felt, though the best gradually tended to be of metal lamellar rather than scale construction. There was probably no uniformity among the Sassanian cavalry elite, each warrior's harness and horse-armour reflecting his own status or wealth.

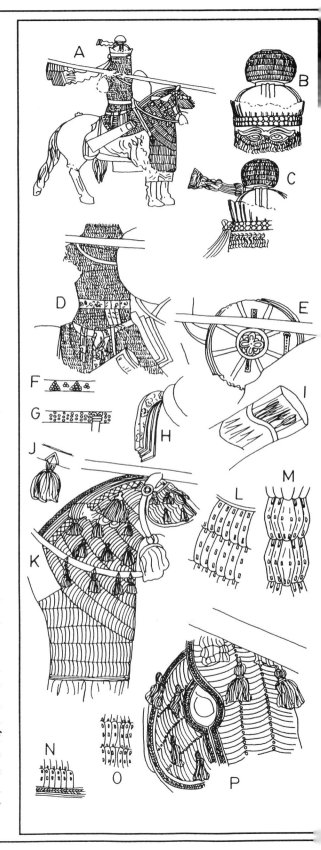

19. Free-standing rock-carved statue, Sassanian early 7th century AD (in situ, Taq-i Bustan, Iran); the last Sassanian military elite.

A The most famous and detailed but also the most untypical representation of a Sassanian cavalryman is the huge statue within the Taq-i Bustan grotto. He has arms, armour and horse-furniture of a type only seen in the last decades of the Sassanian Empire. Nevertheless he reflects the heavy cavalry elite of both late Sassanian armies and those of neighbouring Byzantium, Georgia, Armenia, and those of the first Persian Muslim forces. The only parts of this remarkable statue which are missing are his right arm, though this clearly held his heavy spear level with his shoulders, one of the horse's back legs, its bridle, bit, and the rider's foot. This particularly unfortunate as it is impossible to tell whether he was riding with a stirrup.

B & C Beneath the large pompom, indicating royal status, is a raised crown-like fringe and a knotted bandana which streams to the rear. Within these the rider has a very interesting form of low-domed, segmented and framed helmet. A large face-covering mail aventail is directly attached to the helmet rim, as would be seen in Middle Eastern armour funtil modern times, plus a pair of decorative eyebrows. Close inspection suggests that there might have been a rigid visor below the face-covering mail, though this could merely indicate a padded protective lining.

D The horseman's main protection is a mail hauberk which reaches his knees. The length of the sleeves is unknown and the way in which the hauberk falls over the saddle suggests that the hem was slit in front but not at the back. Around his waist are two belts. The upper one probably had suspension straps to a scabbard on the left hip. It also seems to have three short pendant straps on the right hip; an early Persian example of a military status belt of Turkish origin. The lower belt carries archery equipment, including a new and characteristically Central Asian form of box-like quiver. There also appears to be a cloth kerchief thrust into this belt, just as would be described in military texts from a century or so later. The raised, and in this case stepped, saddle-bow or pommel is clearly visible in front of the rider's thighs. The outline of the hauberk over the rear of his saddle suggests a slightly raised cantle, all of which indicate that he is riding a wood-framed saddle of Central Asian form.

E The medium-sized round shield is barely damaged. It has a guige strap which goes around the man's neck and a decorated but virtually flat boss at the centre. The three short strap-shaped apparently non-functional elements attached to the face of the shield have remarkable parallels in shield decorations found far to the west in early medieval Germanic Europe.

F Detail of the decoration of the upper or presumed sword-belt. This would probably have been made of small bronze, silver or gold studs.

G Detail of the decoration of the lower or archery-belt with the attachment for a strap to support the quiver.

H Front view of the stepped saddle-bow or pommel. The decorative flowers across the surface suggest that it would have been covered in fine-quality cloth as shown on similarly dated wall-paintings and stucco figurines from Transoxania and Chinese Turkestan.

I Upper part of the quiver. Here the carving is remarkably superficial compared to the rest of the statue. Nevertheless it the quiver is clearly of an enclosed box-type which, even in the 14th century AD, would be associated with nomad horse-archers of the Central Asian steppes rather than the armies of the Middle East. This is further evidence of a strong wave of Turkish military influence felt in the Sassanian Empire during its final decades.

J Detail of one of the tassels and its presumed metal holder attached to the horse's reins. Similar tassels are shown on the horse's neck armour and head-protecting chamfron.

K The horse armour of the Taq-i Bustan statue was of a new type which only covers the front of the animal, neck and head. Byzantine military treatises of this period state that such limited horse armour was copied from the invading Avars. Its appearance in late Sassanian Iran shows that the Persians were similarly adopting new military ideas from invading nomads. The armour itself consists of three sheets, two being of metalic lamellar, probably iron and/or bronze. The lamellae of the peytral chest-piece overlapped forwards and upwards. Those of the crinet neck-piece overlapped rearwards and downwards. The crinet also has a series of decorated strips down the top of the neck. These almost certainly represent one or more layers of cloth-covered padding to protect straps or laces which secured the crinet around the neck and provided additional protection for the animal's spine.

L Detail of the upper rows of lamellae of the crinet also showing the edging strip.

M Detail of the central line of lamellae down the front of the crinet showing rows of lamellae overlapping rearwards from a vertical line of larger lamellae.

N Detail of the bottom row of lamellae of the peytral showing a broad band of presumed leather lacing.

O Detail of the central line of lamellae down the front of the peytral showing rows of lamellae overlapping forwards until they meet over a vertical line of presumably larger lamellae.

P The chamfron head-piece of the horse's armour, the third major element, is made in a different manner. It consists of upwards overlapping strips or lames rather than lamellae, perhaps of hardened leather rather than bronze or iron. Each lame is quite long and has a scalloped edge where it is riveted to its neighbour. The entire chamfron is made in three sections covering the front and sides of the head, just as would remain the case throughout the history of medieval Islamic horse-armour. Each of the three sections is edged with a broad strip of presumed leather lacing.

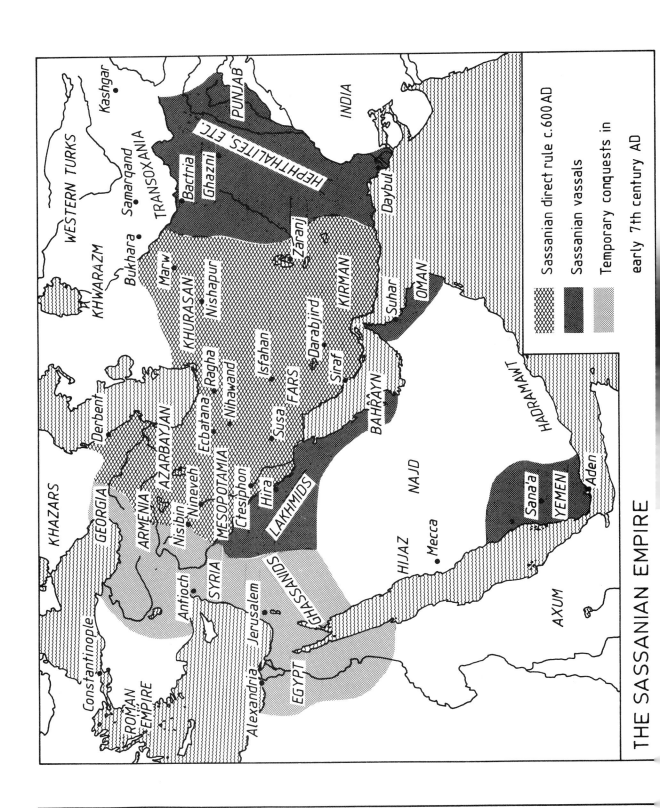

THE SASSANIAN EMPIRE

Sassanian direct rule c.600 AD

Sassanian vassals

Temporary conquests in early 7th century AD

A1. East Parthian cataphract
A2. Parthian horse-archer
A3. Hatrene cataphract

A1
A2
A3

Plate A: The Parthians (2-3 centuries AD)

Plate B: The Rise of the Sassanians (early-mid 3 century AD)

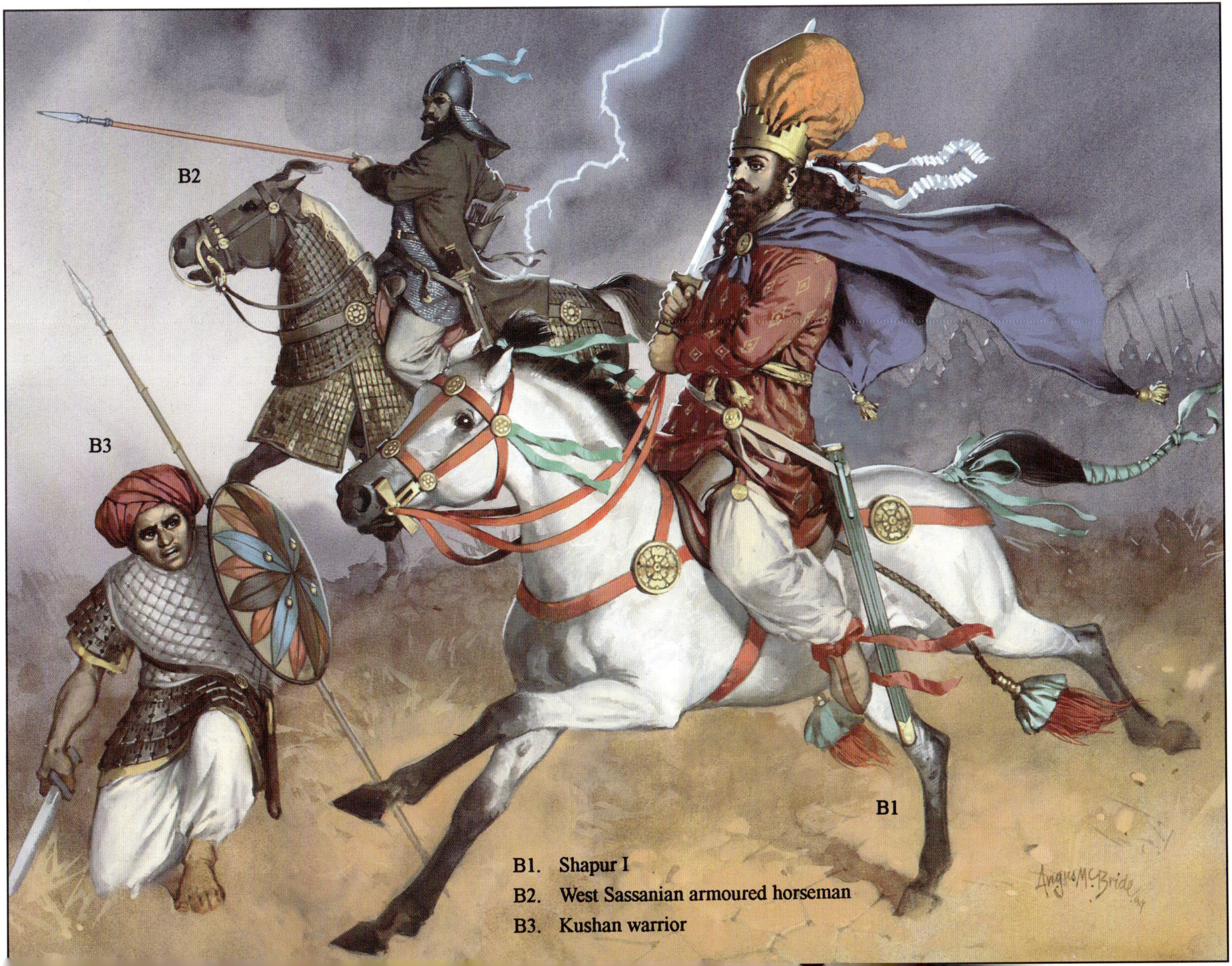
B2
B3
B1
B1. Shapur I
B2. West Sassanian armoured horseman
B3. Kushan warrior
Angus McBride

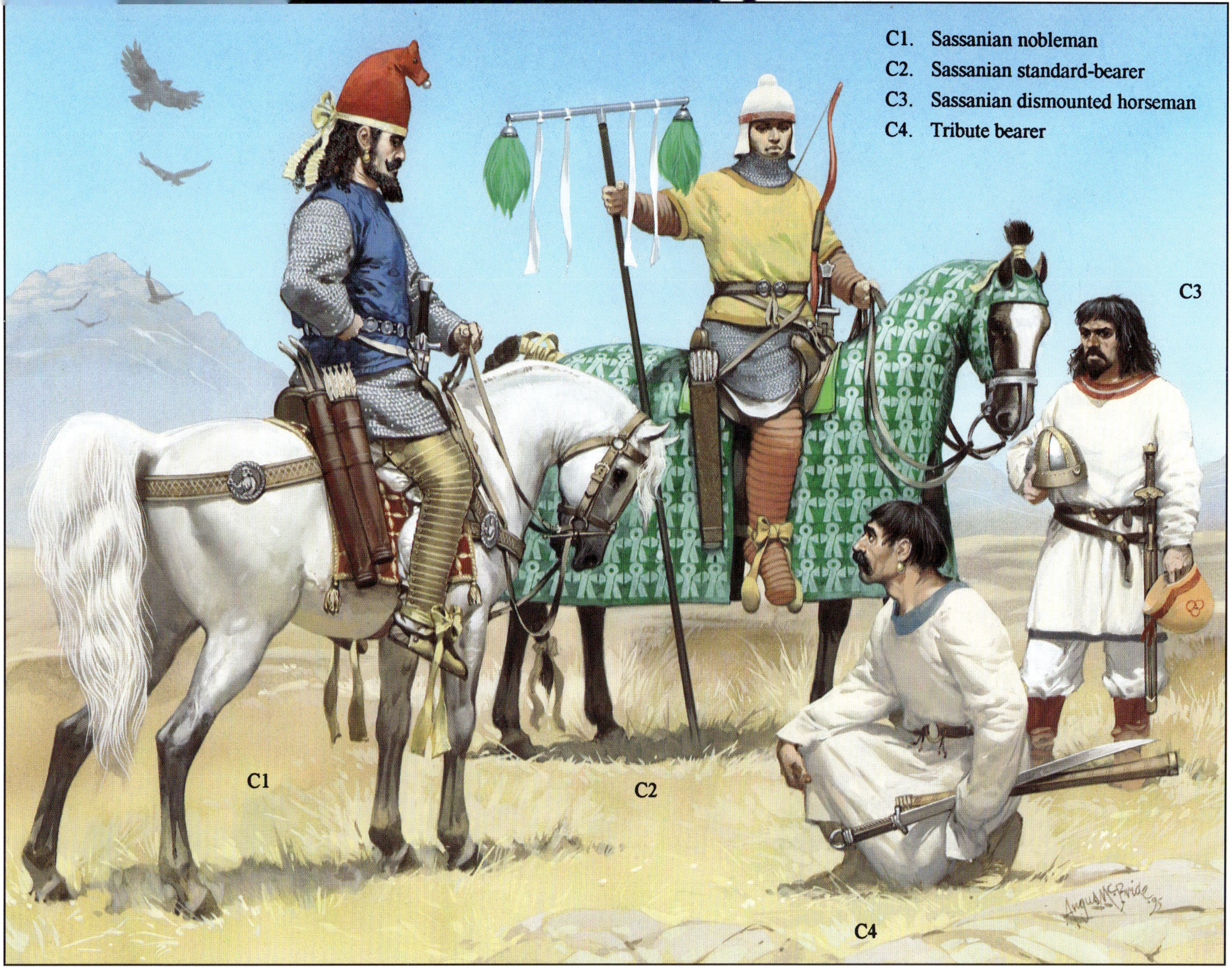

C1. Sassanian nobleman
C2. Sassanian standard-bearer
C3. Sassanian dismounted horseman
C4. Tribute bearer
C1
C2
C3
C4
Angus McBride '95

Plate C: Sassanian Expansion (3-4 centuries AD)

Plate D: The Sassanians face Rome (3-4 centuries AD)

D1. Sassanian Prince
D2. Sassanian soldier
D3. Roman leader
D4. Hormuzd II

D4

D3

D2

D1

E1. East Sassanian warrior
E2. Hun tribal leader
E3. Ephthalite nobleman
E4. Saka warrior

Plate E: The Sassanians face the Huns (5 century AD)

Plate F: Sassanian Royal Hunt (6 century AD)

F1. Elephant and crew
F2. Attendants in *sambuq*
F3. Khusru I

F1.
F2.
F3.

G1. Sassanian *aswaran* in Yemen
G2. *Aswaran* officer in Oman
G3. Arab boy warrior

Plate G: The Sassanians in Arabia (6-7 centuries AD)

Plate H: The fall of the Sassanians (mid-7 century AD)

H1. Sassanian nobleman
H2. Persian light cavalryman
H3. Sassanian Prince
H4. Sughdian warrior

Plate Captions

Plate A: The Parthians (2-3 centuries AD)

A1. East Parthian cataphract (2 century AD)

Archaeological evidence and surviving pictorial sources indicate that the Parthian heavy cavalry elite wore heavy bronze armour. This figure has a scale cuirass and laminated limb defences. His helmet is covered with a felt hat and has an aventail of small bronze scales. As a cataphract close-combat cavalryman he is armed with spear and sword but hangs his archery equipment from his saddle rather than a belt. The man's horse is similarly protected by bronze armour, though here it is of lamellar rather than scale construction. The saddle is of the "horned" type also used by Roman cavalry

A2. Parthian horse-archer (2-3 centuries AD)

Most Parthian horse-archers were completely unarmoured. Bushy "fluffed up" hair seems to have been a Parthian characteristic, along with the powerful composite bow and separate loose leggings for each leg. This man's gold neck torque might indicate aristocratic status. He is also armed with a large dagger or short sword, the scabbard of which is thrust inside his right legging. The bow is of an early form, lacking the angled ears of the subsequent Hunnish bow and being weaker than the medieval Seljuk Turkish bow. Once again the bowcase and quiver are attached to the rear of the saddle.

A3. Hatrene cataphract (early 3 century AD)

The military elite of the semi-independent city state of Hatra on the frontier between the Parthian and Roman empires seems to have been equipped in purely Iranian style, though the bulk of the Hatrene army would have consisted of Arab tribal warriors. The quilted cap worn over his helmet by this man, his quilted tunic over a mail hauberk and the open-fronted fur-trimmed coat, are very Persian but his short sword seems more Arabian. The battle standard is based on a Hatrene carving and seems to owe much more to Roman influence, though the crescent moon near the top is a pre-Islamic Middle Eastern symbol.

Plate B: The Rise of the Sassanians (early-mid 3 century AD)

1. Shapur I (early-mid 3 century AD)

The basic costume of the ruling Sassanian Great King changed little throughout the history of the dynasty. Each ruler had his own distinctive headgear but otherwise his costume was basically the same as that of other members of the military elite. At this time the wearing of elaborate jewelry was also a mark of the aristocracy. The scabbard slide, attached to the outside of the scabbard, was a typical Iranian method of carrying a sword which spread across most of Europe and Asia. It was not superseded by the Central Asian Turkish sword-belt for two or more centuries. The saddle is of the "horned type" also used in Rome, though where it was first developed remains unknown. The decorative cutting of the horse's mane was an Iranian fashion which persisted for many years.

B2. West Sassanian armoured horseman (3 century AD)

This figure is largely based on a body found in one of the Sassanian assault mines beneath Dura Europos. A mail hauberk found on the corpse appeared to be decorated on the chest with a trident motif in bronze mail links. Similar heraldic motifs are seen in several rock-carvings. Apparently the Sassanians made full use of mail armour before the Romans did so. The mail aventail could equally well have included face-covering across the front. The large button which secures the sword belt over the groin was another device of presumed Iranian origin. One interpretation of difficult pictorial sources is to give the figure immensely thick padded kid-leather leggings.

B3. Kushan warrior (3 century AD)

It is interesting to note that a great many pictorial sources from early medieval India and what is now Afghanistan show clear-shaven warriors, whereas most western Sassanian soldiers sport beards or at least moustaches. The turban was also a distinctly eastern feature at this time. The man's armour consists of thickly quilted cotton for the body plus hardened leather scales for the arms and thighs. Archaeological and artistic evidence shows that short swords, comparable to those of the Arab Middle East, were common in northern India.

Plate C: Sassanian Expansion (3-4 centuries AD)

C1. Sassanian nobleman (early-mid 3 century AD)

Mail remained the normal form of armour in the Sassanian heartlands, apparently supplemented by some laminated protections particularly for the legs, while the feet could be protected by metallic slippers. Swords gradually grew longer. This man wears one of the elaborately shaped hats shown in Sassanian rock-carvings. They were probably individual methods of identification for the higher military aristocracy. As he is quite a senior man he has been given a fine bred horse with a decorated saddle, though it is still of the horned type, while the bridle and bit are rather primitive in having large *psalion* cheek-pieces.

C2. Sassanian standard-bearer (3 century AD)
Apart from the attempted reconstruction of a Sassanian battle-standard, this picture also offers another suggested interpretation of the arms and leg coverings shown in early Sassanian rock-relief carvings. Here they consist of thickly quilted fabric. The young warrior's helmet is covered by a cap or hood. This time, however, the man carries his quiver from a belt rather than hanging it from the rear of his saddle. Note that his bow is asymmetrical. The horse's caparison is probably of fabric-covered felt to provide some protection against arrows, and is decorated with "keyhole" heraldic motifs. It is also made in two sections in front and behind the saddle. The bridle and bit are of the framed caveson type.

C3. Sassanian dismounted horseman, or possibly infantryman (3 century AD)
The quality of this man's equipment suggests that he may be a dismounted member of the cavalry elite. His helmet is of the framed Parthian Cap form. This could be worn underneath a decorated cap as shown being held by this man. Beneath his tunic he has a mail hauberk. His sword-belt has been tightened so that the scabbard does not drag along the ground while walking.

C4. Tribute bearer (3 century AD)
Though this man wears much the same basic costume as the other figures he has no armour. One sleeve has also been extended to its full length. The sword he carries as tribute from a neighbouring ruler was found by archaeologists north of the Tien Shan mountains. It has a ring-shaped pommel and two short quillons all forged from the same iron bar as the blade itself.

Plate D: The Sassanians face Rome
(3-4 centuries AD)

D1. Sassanian Prince (4 century AD)
By the 4th century subtle changes were taking place in the very conservative court costume of the Sassanian Empire. The most obvious was the adoption of a system of straps and medallions around the chest to indicate high status. Its origins are obscure but might be found in India. Male jewelry was as obvious as ever and the weapons had not changed much. The horse, however, has a new form of saddle which lacks the old-fashioned "horns" and appears to be built around a simple wooden frame.

D2. Sassanian soldier (3-4 centuries AD)
Infantry never enjoyed high status in the Sassanian Empire. This soldier is perhaps one of a select few in possessing a proper helmet and a mail hauberk which he wears beneath his tunic. With a spear, two small javelins and a shield made of cane and leather he is probably equipped for siege warfare. The two extra rings on his belt appear in several carvings and may have been to suspend other weapons, though they are usually shown only with the two belt-ends threaded through.

D3. Roman leader (4 century AD)
By the later 4th century the Romans were also using various forms of lamellar armour, this captured Roman leader's cuirass being made of the smallest type of stapled bronze lamellae yet found in a Roman site. Rome, like the Sassanian Empire, clung to very conservative features of costume and ceremonial armour, particularly in a courtly context. This would account for the archaic *pteruges* hanging from this man's shoulders and waist.

D4. Hormuzd II (early 4 century AD)
Whereas the costume of the Sassanian prince represents that seen in the late 4th century, the Sassanian Emperor Hormuzd II wears the even more archaic dress of the early 4th century. Again he has his own distinctive headdress or crown, different from that of any other Emperor, while both man and horse appear to have even more dangling ribbons and tassels than usual. This time his long bushy beard is tucked inside a broadened "chin-strap". His massive sword is still suspended from a scabbard slide. We have interpreted the armour he wears beneath a short shirt as a scale cuirass. It might equally well have been of mail.

Plate E: The Sassanians face the Huns
(5 century AD)

E1. East Sassanian warrior (5 century AD)
By the late Sassanian period the military costume of the eastern regions clearly differed from that of the west and of earlier centuries. This resulted from outside influence and invasions, most importantly by the Huns and other Turco-Mongol Central Asian peoples. This aristocratic warrior's hat it very Central Asian in style, the decorative pendants on his belt even more so. They were originally for hanging weapons but gradually came to represent elite military status throughout the Middle East and much of Eastern Europe. His scabbard and quiver are suspended in a new way. In this reconstruction we have given his horse leather loop stirrups. This feature is unproved but appears in some northern Indian art and could be hinted at in other sources.

E2. Hun tribal leader (5 century AD)

Persians, Europeans, Indians and other civilized peoples who found themselves on the receiving end of the Hun invasions all agree that their attackers were a wild, unwashed and barbarous crowd. In military terms, however, the Huns may have enjoyed several technological advantages stemming from the strong Chinese influence on their original Central Asian homeland. Nevertheless this figure has only been given a minimal amount of rudimentary leather lamellar armour. Beneath he is dressed in typical Central Asian costume and carries two unstrung bows. On the other hand his scabbard would seem to indicate that he has captured a fine sword from his Sassanian foes.

E3. Ephthalite nobleman (6-7 centuries AD)

The magnificent and remarkably well preserved wall paintings of pre-Islamic Panjikent and other sites in Transoxania mean that the costume, weaponry and horse-harness of the north-eastern frontier regions of the Sassanian world can be reconstructed in much greater detail than those of the Sassanian capital and its surroundings to the west. These eastern regions were already being colonized by Turks and this was reflected in costume and weapons. A tight cap looks almost Chinese whereas the decorative panels on his tunic are purely Sassanian. His belt, purse, kerchief and dagger are Turkish while his sword is of the "ring pommel" type which may have originated somewhere in Central Asia but eventually also found its way into late Roman armies.

E4. Saka warrior (6 century AD)

The Sakas were nomadic warrior people of Iranian rather than Turkish origin. They saw a brief period of political power along the eastern frontiers of the Sassanian Empire and thereafter seem to have served in the armies of various people, including the Sassanians. With his late form of Sassanian segmented helmet, mail hauberk worn beneath a tunic of the finest Sassanian fabric and weaponry which owes more to Transoxania than to the Sassanian heartlands, this warrior may represent those who put up the final resistance to the advancing Muslim Arabs in eastern Iran. His horse's harness could have been found throughout these eastern regions, but the bright silk cloth over the saddle suggests contact with Chinese dominated eastern Turkestan.

Plate F: Sassanian Royal Hunt (6 century AD)

This plate shows the King of Kings hunting wild boars in the marshes of southern Iraq. Rectangular panels on the side walls at Taq-i Bustan show Khusru II (591-628) in a great hunt. The scene is mapped on to a 9 x 8 set of squares which echoes the playing surface used in a chess-like game called *chatarunga*. Rather than attempt a direct copy, with all the problems that would entail, we have reconstructed a hunt featuring Khusru I (531-579) but with much of the detail still inspired by the aforementioned reliefs.

F1. Elephant and crew for the hunt (6 century AD)

The elephant is reconstructed essentially after the Taq-i Bustan reliefs but a mixture of written, carved and other sources from both Iran and India are corroborative. The reliefs show the dead quarry being carried in the manner depicted here. It is interesting to note that the wild boar often features as a decorative motif on Sassanian clothing. The *mahout*, or elephant driver, could be an Indian or an Iranian. Carvings and other representations of *mahouts* often show them wearing bulky turbans. The rider at the back puts his leg through a rope running beneath the animal's tail, in a manner identical to that used in medieval and later India.

F2. Attendants in *sambuq* (6 century AD)

Hunting on a large scale and in a highly organized manner had been a way of expressing royal power for centuries. Judging by surviving pictorial sources the court and military elite also dressed finely for such events.
The heads on many of the Taq-i Bustan figures are damaged or completely destroyed and it is difficult to decide whether some individuals wear caps or turbans. Seeing as turbans are known from other sources we have opted for them in this instance. In the Taq-i Bustan reliefs some *sambuq* boats have crews larger than shown here.

F3. Khusru I (mid 6 century AD)

The Emperor Khusru I wears the system of decorative straps around his chest. His personally distinctive crown is being held by the man behind him and he wears a low simple form of *qalansuwa* cap such as would be worn in Iran and Iraq for much of the subsequent Islamic period. Though his sword is slung in a more modern manner it still hangs vertically, as does his more old-fashioned quiver.

Plate G: The Sassanians in Arabia (6-7 centuries AD)

G1. Sassanian *aswaran* in Yemen (6-7 centuries AD)
Once again there is more written evidence than pictorial for the Sassanians in pre-Islamic Yemen. The mixed equipment given to this elite cavalryman suggests that he was a second-generation member of the occupation army. The helmet owes as much to early Byzantine equipment as it does to Sassanian, though there is little reason to expect much difference between the two by the late 6th century. His long-sleeved long skirted hauberk is very Arab, though the Arabs themselves probably copied the style from their more advanced neighbours. The hardened leather cuirass, however, seems Arabian and even specifically Yemeni. Leather equipment, including the shield, was certainly manufactured in that region. The horse's harness is based on evidence from both Arabia and Nubia since the written sources suggest cultural and military similarity between both sides of the Red Sea. Elite cavalry of various armies, at this time, normally had a second horse to carry their baggage, as well as one or more servants.

G2. *Aswaran* officer in Oman (6-7 centuries AD)
Since Oman was closer to Iran and had been ruled by the Sassanians or their vassals from Iraq for much longer, this *aswaran* cavalryman has been given more typical late Sassanian equipment. It is quite advanced, consisting of a fine decorated helmet, relatively short mail hauberk, eastern Iranian dagger and sword both in highly decorated silvered scabbards, and a powerful composite bow. The simple vertical open-ended quiver is old-fashioned while the habit of carrying a bow around the neck rather than in a bowcase was typical of Iran but not of Central Asia. The man's saddle is of a wood-framed type such as might now be seen from China to central Europe.

G3. Arab boy warrior (6-7 centuries AD)
Youths and even boys took part in the battles of Sassanian and pre-Islamic Arabia, the future Prophet Muhammad being one. Among other duties they collected spent arrows for re-use. His primitive bow made of bamboo is based on that said to have been owned by the Prophet and now preserved in Istanbul.

Plate H: The fall of the Sassanians (mid-7 century AD)

H1. Sassanian nobleman (mid-7 century AD)
The styles of costume worn by the Sassanian nobility and military elite survived long after the Sassanian Empire was overthrown, and they formed the basis of the court costume of the subsequent Arab Caliphate in Iraq. Once again this man has a simple cap of the qalansuwa type, a long coat or kaftan, and baggy decorated trousers. He might wear large gloves, a new fashion, while the belt, dagger and large straight sword are based on wall paintings from Transoxania. Even the Sassanians' love of male jewelry eventually reappeared in the 9th century AD.

H2. Persian light cavalryman (7 century AD)
Pictorial sources from the very last years of the Sassanian Empire show a quite dramatic shift away from traditional arms and armour to new styles betraying strong Central Asian influence. These include this man's quiver, belt and scabbard-hanging system, probably the sword itself and perhaps even his low-domed framed helmet. There is even evidence of bronze lamellar leg armour being worn beneath his highly decorated gaiters. The saddle with its pronounced pommel is also of a new type but whether true stirrups were widespread among the last Sassanian cavalry remains an open question.

H3. Sassanian Prince (early 7 century AD)
This heavily armoured figure is based almost entirely on the famous rock-cut equestrian statue at Taq-i Bustan dating from the very end of the Sassanian Empire. The only variations are a different sword-belt plus a sash and sword, no archery equipment and the addition of laminated arm-defences such as those shown in wall paintings from Panjikent. He rides with a carved wooden stirrup such as were used in various parts of Central Asia. The feet of the Taq-i Bustan statue are, of course, missing.

H4. Sughdian warrior (7 century AD)
Whereas the preceding figure is based on evidence from western Iran, this man is entirely based on the far more easily interpreted evidence from Transoxania. The directly riveted segmented helmet with a full mail aventail, the long mail hauberk, spear, dagger and large round shield as well as the horse's advanced harness would form the basis of subsequent cavalry equipment in the Middle East. They would also be found in Byzantium, Russia, much of eastern Europe and probably lay behind the development of the heavy cavalry in medieval western Europe. In fact this warrior represents the advanced cavalryman of his day and the future.

Frontier Troops & Fortifications

While the elite of the Sassanian army was stationed near the Court or lived on its own estates, some professional troops were based closer to the frontiers. Many of these were mercenaries forming permanent garrisons under the command of regional governors. Elsewhere the governor of a shahr had his own small bodyguard to maintain order. There were troops garrisoned even in far-flung provinces like Oman on the other side of the Arabian Gulf. Many Persian ships seem to have been manned by coastal Arabs and non-Arab peoples from eastern Arabia. Some of the latter are said to have been descended from Sindi Indian settlers, other from vestigial pre-Semitic probably Hamitic groups. But whether the Sassanian Empire had a navy to maintain communications with its more isolated outposts is unknown.

Closer to the Sassanian capital, the Iraqi frontier had garrisons along the desert fringe, backed up by auxiliary troops recruited from the neighbouring Arab tribes and "client" kings such as the Lakhmids of Hira. As the centuries passed it became clear that the Sassanians were concentrating their military effort in such frontier zones, with very few troops at the centre. By the 6th century the Sassanians were able to field much larger forces than the Romano-Byzantines could along their common frontier in eastern Syria but a century later the Muslim Arabs, once they had defeated the main Sassanian armies in Iraq and Fars, found little to oppose them deeper inside Sassanian territory.

The relationship between the King of Kings and frontier peoples varied according to the fluctuating power of the Empire. The tribal peoples involved were, however, much the same throughout Sassanian history. Some served under their own princes who, with the title of Shathradhars, enjoyed a privileged position at Court. Others were simply paid in silver, and the majority seem to have fought in much the same manner as the Persians. The highest regarded were of Saka nomadic Iranian origin. They came from Sijistan around the Helmand river and lakes in south-western Afghanistan. This area had been dominated by the powerful Suren family in early

Sassanian times but was later placed under imperial governors. Further east was the land of the Kushans, an often rebellious region which, in the mid-4th century, was ruled by Sassanian governors known as Kushanshahs.

Various waves of Hun invaders led to an even more confused situation in these eastern regions during late Sassanian times. The Chionite or Kidarite "Red" Huns arrived in the mid-4th century, the Ephthalite or "White" Huns around 400 AD. Chionites fought for Shapur II under the leadership of their own kings while the Ephthalites, after being defeated by invading Turks in the mid-6th century, retained control of a small area around Kabul until the end of the Sassanian period. The wide-ranging but largely unrecorded 6th century wars between Sassanians and Turks feature in the 10th century Persian Shahnamah epic and seem to have taken place between Sijistan and India in what is now southern Afghanistan - an area the Shahnamah refers to as Turan, "The Land of the Turks". Some princes of Turkish origin seem to have acknowledged Sassanian overlordship in the east, or at least to have fought as allies. There was still a Turkish cavalry elite in this region when the Arabs arrived at the end of the 7th century. The Turks would, in fact, prove to be by far the most important military group in what had been the eastern parts of the Sassanian Empire.

Turkish princes clearly dominated Transoxania and much of northern Afghanistan before the Muslim conquest. Those who ruled the rich commercial cities of Transoxania already had as close contacts with Chinese civilization as with Iran, and their military influence throughout the late Sassanian Empire was greater than is generally realized.

Among other warrior peoples serving the Sassanians as auxiliary troops were Dailamite infantry from the Elburz mountains, and Gels from south-west of the Caspian sea who fought as cavalry. The Sassanian Empire also occupied much of Armenia in the later 4th century, that country finally being divided between the Romano-Byzantines and Sassanians in 428 AD. The Armenian military aristocracy thereafter played a leading role in the armies of various Middle Eastern powers throughout the Middle Ages, fighting as cavalry. The Arab population of Khuzistan, east

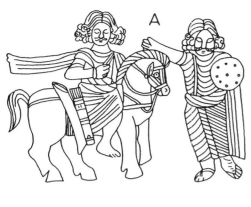

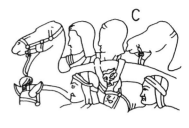

20. The Borderlands: Northern Arabia. A great deal of the fighting which took place along the Sassanian Empire's frontier with the Roman Empire was done by local troops, auxiliaries and allies. The most important were warlike Arab tribes of this frontier region and the desert-steppes to the south.

A Limestone relief carving from Dura Europos, mid-3rd century AD. This simple but stylish carving shows the pre-Islamic pagan gods Asadu and Sa'dai who shared responsibility for the protection of caravans. Both figures have bushy hair characteristic of Parthian and early Arab warriors. They wear long flowing tunics, one clearly opening down the front, and cloaks or *izar* body wrappers. The standing figure carries a small round shield but no visible weapons and wears sandals. The horseman rides barefoot without stirrups, as would still be shown in early 8th century AD Arab-Islamic art. He has a simple open-ended quiver and an apparently empty bowcase for an unstrung bow, both seemingly attached to his saddle rather than hanging from a belt. Most interesting of all, his horse has a standing martingale strap running from its bridle, beneath a breast-strap, to the front of the saddle rather than to the girth as in modern standing martingales. This device stopped a horse tossing its head and would obviously be useful to a horse-archer. But it very rarely appears in the true homeland of horse-archery, Central Asia. Martingales are, however, frequently shown in the art of Syria and neighbouring Arab regions (National Museum, Damascus, Syria).

B Basalt relief carving from the Aleppo region, northern Syria, 2nd or 3rd centuries AD. Carvings in hard volcanic basalt rarely achieve the detail of those in limestone. This strangely proportioned rider and horse are really a form of folk art and represent another pagan god of pre-Islamic Syria. The man's hairstyle and tunic show Mediterranean rather than Iranian influence, but with his spear, round shield and quiver attached to the rear of his saddle, he reflects tribal and other cavalry which fought wars of raid and counter-raid between the Sassanian and Romano-Byzantine Empires (private collection).

of Basra at the head of the Gulf, were also noted horse soldiers. But this area was close to the heart of the Sassanian Empire and to the vulnerable Arabian frontier, having many permanently garrisonned fortresses and fortified arsenals. Other fortifications were established in lower Iraq to store equipment for the Sassanian awaran heavy cavalry and for the troops of the vassal Lakhmids.

Unlike their Parthian predecessors the Sassanians were skilled siege engineers who made considerable use of field fortifications. Eurocentric historians had assumed they learned such skills from the Romans but it is clear that, in many ways, the Sassanians' neighbours in Transoxania, with their close Chinese contacts, were more advanced than European military engineers. The traditional Sassanian siege method was to approach an enemy citadel with trenches protected by wattle mantlets, then to attack its walls with mining, rams, wooden towers and stone-throwing ballistae. The new counterweight mangonel, invented in China, reached Transoxania no later than the early 7th century and it is possible that the Sassanian army attacking Jerusalem around this time already used such machines. They almost certainly defended the Sassanian capital Ctesiphon with them against the Muslims a few years later.

Fortresses featured prominently in **Sassanian** military planning, those near stategic frontiers being commanded by a senior officer sometimes known as a *dyzpt*. Unlike the Romans with their great city walls, the Sassanians appear to have based their defences upon a tower or citadel. Many towns, though not apparently those distant from the frontier zones, had walled citadels. This would have been particularly true of the many "Royal" cities founded by Sassanian Emperors to serve as military headquarters and garrison centres. Some Sassanian cities revived the ancient round plan while others used a grid plan which, however, reflected ancient Indian rather than Graeco-Roman influence. Sassanian garrison cities could, in fact, range from an extensive shahristan with a citadel and suburbs surrounded by a circuit wall, as seen in the militarized eastern provinces, to the small triangular Qala'at al Kisra "Khusru's Castle" perched on a rocky outcrop overlooking the oasis of Rustaq in Oman.

Even more characteristic of Sassanian defensive works, and of the Empire's growing "Maginot Line Mentality", was a series of long-walls along vulnerable frontiers. The primary function of these walls was to stop raiders and nomads entering cultivated zones. In some places they could also keep back drifting desert sand. The fertile area of Gurgan was, for example, defended by the Sadd-i Iskander "Alezander's Barrier" in Persian, or Qizil Yilan "Red Snake" in Turkish. It consisted of a ditch and brick wall running for 170 kms from the Caspian sea to the mountains, probably constructed as part of a great defensive system devised by Yazdagird II or Peroz as a defence against the Huns. An even longer wall may once have extended all the way to the main Sassanian military base at Marw. A shorter wall ran from the Caspian coast to Tammisha as a second line of defence. Other long walls surrounded Marw oasis, Bukhara oasis, and from the Zarafshan river to Samarqand in Transoxania. To the west a wall was erected along the Elburz foothills to stop Daylamite raiders from the mountains. The most famous of all these Sassanian walls was, however, the Bab al Abwab "Gate of Gates" built between the Caspian and the Caucasus mountains near Darband. Legend maintained that it was built by Alexander the Great, though in reality the remains of five separate wall

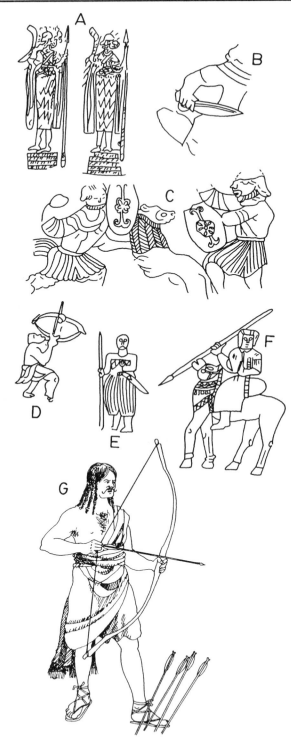

A Carved stone relief, southern Yemen, several centuries pre-Islamic. The two near identical figures of unnamed deities on this carved stele at the entrance to a pagan temple are dressed in a southern Arabian or Yemeni style. It was very different from that of the central or northern Arabs but their long fluffed up hair and decorative crossbelts across their chests might reflect Iranian influence. Both figures carry large-bladed spears while that on the left also seems to have a large curved dagger through a belt or sash. It looks remarkably like the curved daggers still worn by Yemeni men in traditional costume (in situ, Temple of 'Attar, Kharibat al Ati, Yemen).

B & C Relief carving from Zafar, Yemen 3rd century AD. These figures on a carved arch again show how Yemeni costume and weaponry differed from that of northern Arabia. One damaged figure carries a short apparently single-edged leaf-shaped sword with its closest contemporary parallels in India. Yemen had, of course, close trading links with the sub-continent and imported the hindi or Indian sword blades. The two other figures fighting a lion may originally have wielded spears and their oval or near-rectangular shields seem to reflect those of Roman soldiers (Archaeological Museum, Sana'a, Yemen).

D Relief carving on a stone door, Hadramawt 2nd or 3rd centuries AD. This small and damaged figure offers two interesting pieces of information. He wears only the simple loin-cloth associated with Arabian nomads rather than the settled peoples of southern Arabia and also appears to be barefooted. Furthermore he hunts with a large bow whose shape does not indicate a composite construction. Pre-Islamic and early Islamic Arab warriors often fought as archers, but normally on foot rather than horseback. Their bows seem to have been of all-wood construction though this could be of several pieces glued together rather than the primitive single-stave English longbow (in situ, Husn al 'Urr, Yemen).

E Relief carving, Yemen, several centuries pre-Islamic. Even a very simple carving such as this can shed light on the costume and military equipment of Yemen shortly before or during the Sassanian occupation. The warrior is armed with a short spear and a single-edged, slightly curved sword with what appears to be an angled sabre-style grip (Archaeological Museum, Sana'a, Yemen).

F Relief carving, Yemen, several centuries pre-Islamic. Another highly stylized carving illustrates a man on horseback, rather than riding a camel as some interpreters have believed. He is armed with a spear which he wields overarm with one hand. The saddle is not visible but the horse has a breast-strap and no breeching straps. It also has several decorative collars and a fully developed bridle, though no bit is shown. This probably reflects the crudity of the carving though it is also possible that some early Arab horsemen, like their distant descendants, rode using a *bozal* or bitless bridle (Archaeological Museum, Sana'a, Yemen).

G Reconstruction of a pre-Islamic Arab infantry archer based on the relief carving from Husn al 'Urr.

21. The Borderlands: Yemen. The Yemen is the most fertile and populous part of the Arabian peninsula with its own ancient urban civilization. It controlled access between the Red Sea and Indian Ocean hence both the Romano-Byzantines and the ultimately victorious Sassanians wanted to control it.

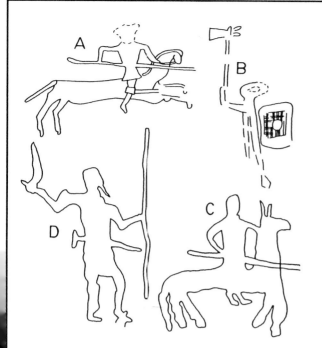

22. The Borderlands: Central Arabia. For thousands of years central Arabia remained a marginal area with a small population and no political power. Nevertheless it was strategically important enough for the rival Sassanian and Romano-Byzantine Empires to compete for control. This they usually did through Arab allies rather than direct conquest. It was also from this unpromising area that a vigorous new civilization would soon emerge, a civilization which would sweep away the Sassanians.

A   Fragments of wall painting, central Arabia 1st to 5th centuries AD. Two quite separate styles of wall painting have been found in one location in pre-Islamic central Arabia. One is highly realistic, the other shown here is exceptionally primitive. This fragment illustrates a horseman wielding a long spear with both hands and apparently wearing some kind of short tunic. Though no saddle is shown, the presence of a breast-strap indicates that the man was not riding bareback. The figure's head has been totally defaced (in situ, Qaryat al Fau, Saudi Arabia).

B   Another primitive fragment of wall painting from the same location, again with the face erased, shows a man on foot with a large axe or flag. He carries a rectangular shield with a central boss which appears to be of the woven cane variety strengthened or edged with a strip of leather, that was used in the Middle East for centuries (in situ, Qaryat al Fau, Saudi Arabia).

C   A third and even simpler wall-painting or graffito from the market area of Qaryat al Fau is believed to have been made during the same period. Here, however, the horseman thrusts his spear using only one hand (in situ, Qaryat al Fau, Saudi Arabia).

D   Petraglyph (picture "pecked" on a rock face using a sharp object such as a stone), central Arabia 1st to 5th centuries AD. There are hundreds of petraglyphs on boulders, cliff-faces and escarpments throughout the desert regions of Arabia from Oman in the east to southern Palestine in the west. This example is unusual because it has an associated inscription which names the subject as one of the pre-Islamic pagan gods, "Kahl the Wise". He has a long beard but lacks the bushy hair seen on northern Arabia gods. In addition he has a short tunic above the knees, a long spear and what might be a short single-edged sword in his right hand. Slung horizontally across his waist is a large dagger or a sword. The traditional male costume of many parts of the Arabian peninsula still includes daggers carried in a similar manner (in situ, Tuwaiq escarpment near Qaryat al Fau, Saudi Arabia).

systems all date from the mid-5th to mid-6th century Sassanian period.

A comparable system could be found in southern Iraq where the concept of long defensive walls was very ancient. One section was known as the Khandaq Shapur "Shapur's Ditch" and consisted of a moat with a rampart. The key position was Anbar which served as an assembly point at the northern end of the rampart, while to the south were regularly spaced towers and fortified outposts running across the plain of Kufa. Another defence ran through Hit to the Gulf coast south of Basra. Like the comparable Roman system of limes in Syria, these walls were defended by local Arab auxiliaries in return for tax exemption. Whereas the Sassanian Empire's eastern and northern walls were well maintained, those facing Arabia were allowed to decay - and it was from Arabia that the Empire's final doom came.

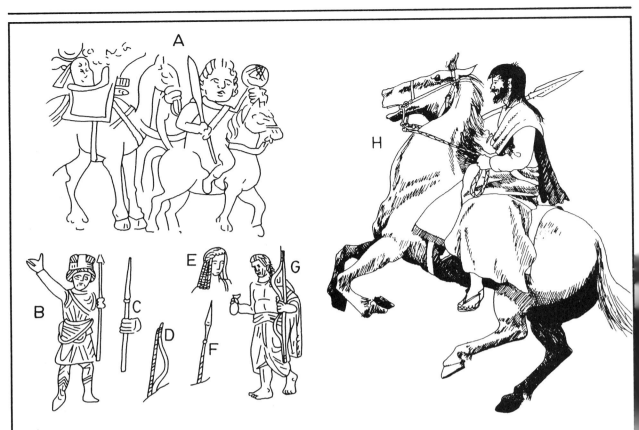

23. The Borderlands: Arabian Warriors in Egyptian Art. Fortunately the crude and simplified art of Arabia can be supplemented with that of its neighbours, many of whom portrayed Arab warriors in considerable detail. This was particularly true of Egypt where, as Christians, the Copts often incorporated bedouin nomads in illustrations of the Old Testament "Story of Joseph".

A Carved limestone relief, Coptic 6th century AD. This is believed to illustrate the "Story of Joseph", the young Hebrew probably being tucked into the camel's howdah on the left. The Midianite Arab who leads the camel is armed with a short-hafted weapon with a massive blade. This is associated with Arab warriors in a much Coptic art and could have been a harbah heavy javelin or short slashing weapon. He may also carry a small round shield. Most interesting of all is the fact that this man rides side-saddle! In modern times, at least in western Europe, such a method of riding was reserved for women in long skirts, but it also appears in an 8th century Transoxanian wall painting of a presumed early Arab-Islamic dignitary. In fact it may stem from a particularly Arab way of avoiding fatigue when riding long distances without the use of stirrups. It was also a normal way of riding a camel (Coptic Museum, Cairo, Egypt).

B Carved ivory situla, Coptic 6th or 7th centuries AD. Here an even clearer representation of an Arab warrior probably formed part of the Joseph story. At this period Byzantine writers habitually described their desert neighbours as "long haired Saracens", though this man's hair is bushy in the old Parthian style. His costume includes a simple head-cloth or bandana, a tunic with a perhaps confused portrayal of a broad cloth waist-wrapper, and boots. He again carries a short hafted weapon, though this time with a small blade (British Museum, London, England).

C to G Carved ivory panels from the Throne of Archbishop Maximian, Coptic c.550 AD. The "Story of Joseph" illustrated in these ivory panels includes accurate and detailed representations of nomadic Arab pre-Islamic tribal warriors. This time the Midianites certainly fit the standard Byzantine description of "long-haired Saracens". Their voluminous *izar* body-wrappers which also go over one arm or shoulder are clearly predecessors of the Muslim's simple *ihram* pilgrim garb as seen every year during the great Islamic Hajj or pilgrimage to Mecca. The weapons consist of a short-hafted large-bladed spear-like object (C), very large recurved bows of probable all-wood construction (D & G), and a large-bladed spear on what seems to be a bamboo haft (F) (Diocesan Museum, Ravenna, Italy).

H Reconstruction of an Arab warrior riding side-saddle, based on the relief carving in the Coptic Museum, Cairo.

Military Reforms in the Later Sassanian Army

A series of defeats at the hands of Huns and other invaders led to a fundamental restructuring of the Sassanian military system in the late 5th century. It was begun by Kavad and completed by Khusru I. A new type of army then defended the Sassanian Empire for another century and a half. Although it then failed against the rising power of the Muslim Arabs, it would have a profound impact upon the tactics, organization, equipment and attitudes of subsequent Islamic armies.

Essentially the 5th century reforms tried to divide society into three separate groups: *arteshtaran* warriors, religious hierarchy and civilian administrators. Nevertheless the main division remained that between the free citizen of supposed "Aryan" descent and the non-citizen non-free "non-Aryan". The *Vuzurg Framadhar* Grand Vizier had increased in importance but had lost his military responsibilities to the *Iran-Spahbad* Commander-in-Chief. Now the Commander-in-Chief was himself replaced by four permanent regional *Spahbads* in charge of one of four frontier regions: Khurasan in the east, Azarbayjan in the north, Fars in the south and Iraq in the west.

24. Sassanian & Allied troops in Egyptian textiles.

A - E Coptic textile, 5th to 7th centuries AD. One remarkable fragment of a larger textile, perhaps originally a wall-hanging, illustrates a battle between a cavalry army and a mixed force of black African warriors and long-haired Arabs. This scene is thought to represent a Sassanian victory, perhaps the Persian conquest of southern Arabia where their enemies would have been the pro-Byzantine Ethiopians and local Arab supporters. If such an identification is correct then this Coptic textile might have been made during the short-lived Sassanian occupation of Egypt early in the 7th century AD. The two dismounted horse-archers at the top of the scene wear long-sleeved mail hauberks. The undamaged right-hand figure has a quiver on his right hip and a bowcase on his left. Both these archers shoot at enemies hiding in a stylized hill or rocky outcrop. On the left of the middle register is another presumed unarmoured Sassanian horse-archer making a "Parthian shot" at a long-haired Arab warrior who carries a round shield. On the right a more damaged horseman blows a triumphant blast on a trumpet while leading a captive African by a rope around his neck. This African carries a very large sword in a scabbard slung from a baldric in the Byzantine and early Arab manner. A bearded figure apparently wearing a mail hauberk and resting his hands on the pommel of a straight sword sits below the battle on an elaborate throne. He might represent the victorious Sassanian commander or King of Kings (Textile Museum, Lyons, France).

F - H Coptic textile, 7th century AD. Another textile illustration of the "Story of Joseph" might have been made shortly after the collapse of the Sassanian Empire when Byzantine Egypt had fallen to the Muslim Arabs. The figures are much more stylized and the Midianite is shown with a pointed hat or helmet over a head-cloth which, on two of the figures, runs beneath his chin. On one occasion the Midianite also carries what looks like a simple round-headed mace or club, a lightweight weapon given to nomads and other specifically Arab figures in medieval Islamic art (State Hermitage Museum, St. Petersburg, Russia).

25. The Borderlands: The Caucasus. The Arch of Galerius, late Roman 297-311 AD. Armenia and Georgia lay between the Romano-Byzantine and Sassanian Empires. Sometimes they were independent, sometimes accepting the suzereinty of one empire and sometimes directly ruled either. Armenia and Georgia eventually became Christian kingdoms though linguistically they had more in common with Iran than with Greeks and Romans to the west. A third area, subsequently known as Azarbayjan, would eventually evolve into a Turkish-speaking Muslim province though not until long after the fall of the Sassanians. The carvings on the Arch of Galerius not only provide excellent evidence of late Roman cavalry equipment. They also portray various of the Roman Empire's eastern neighbours. It was the Sassanian ruler Narseh's reoccupation of Armenia which prompted the ferocious war with Rome, celebrated on the Arch of Galerius.

A & B The main events in these high-relief carvings are the defeat of Narseh's army in Armenia in 297AD and Galerius' subsequent "Triumph" . Included in the latter were Narseh's captured family and Sassanian nobles accompanied by camels and elephants. The accuracy with which these animals are shown indicates that the man who designed the carvings was working from first-hand sketches or even live models. Thus one may assume that the costume of the captured Persians and their various unidentified allies is equally accurate.

C & D Here the rout of the Sassanian army in the mountains of Armenia includes several different types of Persian or Armenian troops. The most commonly shown are probably standard Sassanian unarmoured light cavalry. They wear forward-tilted Phrygian caps, knee-length tunics with decorated hems and in most cases long sleeves, plus long baggy trousers. Several have cloaks secured by large brooches. They are armed with relatively short swords and carry large decorated oval shields.

E Very few Sassanian troops on the Arch of Galerius wear armour. Those that do so have scale or mail shirts similar to, though shorter than, those worn by the Roman heavy cavalry cataphracts in the same carvings. This particular figure has a peculiar hat or helmet that might reflect the two-piece construction of a form of mid-3rd century AD Sassanian helmet excavated at Dura Europos. Generally speaking this type of armoured warrior is probably the least reliable of all those Sassanians included on the Arch of Galerius.

F One group of warriors demands particular attention. They are undoubtedly "enemies" as they are shown in combat with Romans. They are also relatively undamaged. On the left a stricken man appears to have "Aethiopian" or African features and long hair, perhaps representing what the Roman or Greek artist though to be an Arab. To the right a ...

25. (cont.)

... cavalryman attempts to defend himself with a spear thrust with one hand. He seems to wear a low cap rather than a helmet but certain details of his shoulder and belt strongly suggest that he has some form of body armour. In front of him stand two well preserved infantrymen wearing different but certainly un-Roman helmets. That in the centre is similar to the cloth hood or cap-covered helmets worn by almost all early Byzantine troops in art of the 6th to 8th centuries AD. This Byzantine habit of wearing a cloth covering over a helmet was itself of Persian, Caucasian and ultimately perhaps Central Asian origin. The foot soldier on the far right might also have a cap over his helmet; either this or the helmet itself has a broad chin-strap. Both infantrymen have short scale or mail cuirasses such as those seen on a few other Sassanian in this carving, and they have long striped skirts similar to the groin-protecting strips of earlier Roman infantry. One clearly has thick puttee-like bindings around his legs; again a feature which would become common in subsequent Byzantine illustrations of soldiers. This man is armed with a heavy sling and both infantrymen carry large shields of a type which had become old-fashioned in the Roman army. The precise identification of these men is unknown, but their mixture of antiquated Roman and more modern Iranian equipment suggests that they may represent Armenians from the frontierlands between the Roman and Sassanian Empires (in situ, Arch of Galerius, Thessaloniki, Greece).

G   Reconstruction of an Armenian infantryman based on the Arch of Galerius in Thessaloniki.

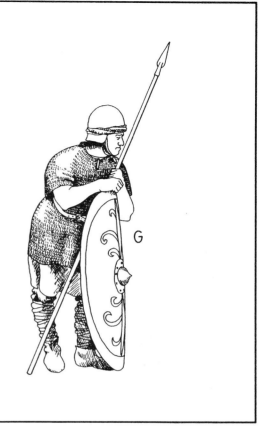

The defence structure of these four regions was also reorganized with particularly importance being given to Khurasan and Iraq to guard against Turks and Huns from one direction, Romano-Byzantines and their Arab vassals from the other. The system soon proved its worth, though the central regions of the Empire were virtually denuned of garrisons. Sometimes the four new frontier governors were still called *Marzbans*, though in general this title now refered to governors of less important smaller central provinces. Under the new system only the four great frontier *Spahbads* were allowed to enter camp to the sound of trumpets. They almost certainly had their own standing forces to guard the frontier and maintain order. A large force of Daylamites from the personal army of the *Spahbad* of Iraq were, in fact, among the first Sassanian professional troops to enlist in the Muslim army. During a major campaign the King of Kings might place an *Arteshtarasalar* in overall command of more than one *Spahbad's* army. Meanwhile an *Aswaran Sardar* commanded the elite cavalry.

Before Khusru's reforms the *dihqan* lesser gentry had declined in military importance compared to the private armies of great Sassanian nobles. Now, however, their fortunes revived and *dihqans* of both Iranian and Semitic Aramaean origin were moulded into a new and highly influential "nobility of service". These professional soldiers owed loyalty directly to the ruler and were, for the first time, paid and armed directly by central government. But since cash payment was not enough to support such well-armed cavalry the *dihqans* were also granted the rents of villages as fiefs. Other military families were given land near the frontiers and were expected to be ready to fight at short notice. In these ways *dihqans* remained the backbone of the Sassanian state until the Muslim conquest.

The King of Kings naturally still had his own guard units, often named after the ruler who enlisted them such as "Khusru's Own" and the *Perozitae*. Some senior military leaders also seem to have had guard units, general Sahen leading the "Golden

26. The Borderlands: The Caucasus. Eastern Prisoners and Tribute-bearers in Late Roman art.

A The lost Column of Arcadius, late Roman c.400 AD, Istanbul; from a Renaissance drawing of the carved reliefs on the base of this Column made before its collapse. In this traditional and only superficially Christianized Roman "Triumph" several prisoners and their weaponry are brought forward by a pagan Victory figure. In reality the reign of Arcadius was one of disaster for the Roman Empire, though relations between Romans and Sassanians remained cordial since both were threatened by barbarian invasion. Hence the presence of "eastern" figures wearing Phrygian caps and perhaps the shaggy sheep-skin coats traditionally associated with Armenians and Persians in Arcadius' undeserved Triumph scene was merely symbolic (Drawing of lost Column of Arcadius, Trinity College Library, Cambridge, England).

B Relief carving, late Roman c.390 AD. The presence of Tribute-bearers on the base of the Obelisk of Theodosius the Great is more justified and certainly easier to interpret. Armenia had already been peacefully partitioned between Romans and Sassanians, each half ruled by the ancient Armenian Arsacid dynasty under foreign suzereinty. The figures shown here are probably Armenians, though they could also be Georgians, both peoples being shown in their own and neighbouring art wearing large fur cloaks with long empty sleeves (in situ, Obelisk of Theodosius the Great, Istanbul, Turkey).

Lances" in 625 AD. But still the Empire was short of indigenous military manpower and Khusru enlisted Abkhazians, Khazars, Alans and other foreigners, some of whom were prisoners of war. Many were sent to fight for the four frontier *Spahbads*, and on other occasions entire populations were forcibly moved from one frontier zone to another. Even so the situation had got so bad that, in 625 AD, the Sassanian ruler tried to raise an army from ordinary civilians, slaves and resident foreigners - it was a failure.

Tactically the later Sassanian army did not change though there was a rise in the importance of horse-archery, Hun and Turkish influence leading to the re-adoption of the bow as a war rather than hunting weapon for the cavalry elite. There may also have been a brief Avar influence upon the last Sassanian forces following military cooperation against the Byzantines in the early 7th century. Nevertheless Persian archery still emphasised the speed rather that the power of shooting, 6th and 7th century Byzantine and Arab archers still using more powerful bows than the Sassanians.

Meanwhile heavily armoured *aswaran* shock cavalry remained the most important troops, the most completely armoured being called *tanurigh* "over men" because of the weight of their equipment. A description of such a heavy cavalryman was preserved in the work of the Persian-Arab historian, al Tabari He (Khusru I) insisted that every man present himself completely protected with a mail hauberk and over this a (lamellar) cuirass reaching his knees, a helmet on his head with an aventail, plus iron vambraces for both arms. The horse should similarly be covered with a bard. Each man was to have a spear, sword, shield (perhaps a later anachronism) and a belt around his waist from which attached an iron mace (perhaps another later anachronism) which dangled at the front of his saddle. Behind the saddle was a quiver containing sixty wooden arrows. On the left side was the bowcase containing two bows, each with its string. He also had two spare strings, in case of breakage in combat, attached to the saddle-bow.

The political consequences of Khusru's reform was less successful than the immediate military consequences. The ruler now relied on his Court bureaucracy and the new *dihqans* "nobility of service". The old sub-kings virtually vanished and the power of the great noble families had been greatly reduced along with their private armies as the Sassanian Empire became more centralized. Under a strong ruler this made the Royal Court very effective, but under a weak ruler it led to disintegration. The old noble families resisted reform until the very end of the Sassanian state and the new "nobility of service" gradually won a degree of independence from central government. The Empire became increasingly militarized and was eventually dominated by powerful military leaders such as the four great *Spahbads* whose huge frontier territories became semi-independent hereditary fiefs.

Military defeats then undermined the prestige of the Sassanian Emperor and his army, particularly in Arabia where a great deal of Sassanian weaponry fell into the hands of the tribes. Even before the Muslim invasion of Iraq in the 7th century, pre-Islamic Arab tribes had raided deep into Sassanian territory. These tribes then attached themselves to the Muslims as auxiliaries when the final crisis came.

During the last decades of the Sassanian Emperor the King of Kings had little control over Herat in the east or Daylam in the north. Elsewhere frontier princes adopted royal titles of Persian or Turkish origin. After the Iraqi frontier had been overrun and the armies of the Court defeated, other provincial military leaders like the *Marzban* of Khurasan seemed unwilling to unite against the common foe. Even so Sassanian troops clearly put up a fierce fight; so much so that they were immediately welcomed into the conquering Muslim Arab army as soon as they converted to Islam. A great many did so and, known as *hamra* or the "red-faced ones", often got higher pay than ordinary Arab soldiers. They included *dihqans* of the local minor aristocracy as well as Daylamite infantry from the northern mountains. In fact it seems that ex-Sassanian troops were entrusted with the defence of the expanding Muslim frontier in central Iran while the main Arab army remained in the newly created Muslim garrison town of Kufa in Iraq, only being used for major expeditions.

Vassal Armies

In many cases the situation of frontier peoples changed during the course of Sassanian history and at the same time there was strong Sassanian influence far beyond the borders of the Empire itself. The eastern frontiers could be divided into four distinct zones. Each of these zones could be considered to have its own cultural characteristics: Balkh in northern Afghanistan was strongly Buddhist and retained many earlier Kushan features; Herat in western Afghanistan was largely Zoroastrian and Sassanian in culture; Zabulistan in central Afghanistan was largely pagan with strong Hindu elements; the Kabul area in eastern Afghanistan included a thriving Buddhist community and was very Indian in culture. These were also warlike areas and after the collapse of the Sassanians, Zabulistan and the Kabul region put up a stiffer resistance to the Muslim Arabs than did other parts of what had been the Sassanian Empire.

In complete contrast the rich cities of Sughd in Transoxania soon recognized the advantages of forming part of a vast new empire centred upon the commercially-minded Arab states of the Middle East and stretching from Western Europe to the borders of China. During the Sassanian period the Sughdians had developed close contacts with China and there were many Sughdian settlers in the Ordos region of northern China, including soldiers as well as merchants. Those who settled in oases along the famous Silk Road linking China with the west also served as cultural, religious and military advisors to successive Great Turk, Western Turk and Eastern Turk rulers. Others colonized the Semirechye region north of the Tien Shan mountains while to the south, in the foothills of the Kun Lun mountains, long-established Buddhist Iranian populations maintained close links with China, Tibet and India. It is hardly surprising that advanced forms of Chinese military technology were known in Transoxania in late Sassanian times.

Nevertheless Sughdia and other parts of Transoxania were no mere reflections of Sassanian Iran or China. A whole new civilization has been discovered by archaeologists which, despite obvious Sassanian parallels, had a distinctive military organzation. From the 2nd to 5th centuries AD the power of nomadic groups declined while that of cities grew. In the 6th century the ruling Turkish elite adopted Buddhism almost as a national faith in contrast to Iranian Zoroastrianism or Chinese Confusianism. Though often forced to accept Sassanian overlordship, local rulers tried to emphasize their own identity, each having a distinctive golden throne mounted on carved animals - a ram in Farghana, a camel in Bukhara. A specifically Transoxanian form of military unit was the *chakir* bodyguards of local lords and leading merchants. These troops not only served as soldiers but managed their employer's business affairs when he was away. The *chakir* may also have been the basis of a subsequent Muslim system of *mamluk* trusted soldiers of slave-origin.

Five small kingdoms dominated many other petty rulers in this area when the Muslims arrived. One was a woman, the *Khatun* of Bukhara, with her own well-armoured guards drawn from local Turkish nobles and the minor Iranian nobility of *dihqans*. The *dihqans* now seem to have been even more important in Sughdia than in the heartlands of the Sassanian Empire, some having their own small castles. Similarly there were already many Turks in the eastern parts of Iran itself, including miners as well as mercenaries.

On the north-western frontier of the Empire the kingdoms of Armenia and Georgia were often allies and occasional vassals of the King of Kings, yet their lands were never considered part of *Iranshahr*. The military elite of both countries continued to be as influenced by the Sassanians as by their Byzantine neighbours, even after they became Christian.

Militarily more important were Arab peoples of the south-western frontier, most though not all of whom were nomadic bedouin. The Kingdom of Ahwaz, for example, had been virtually independent under the Parthians and was not placed under direct Sassanian rule until the mid-3rd century. It had a fully armoured cavalry elite comparable to that of the Sassanians . Others vassal armies of the frontier zone similarly modelled themselves on Sassanians rather than Romans.

27. The Borderlands: Armenia & Georgia; later relief carvings.

A   Duke Stephanos I of Iberia, Georgian relief-carving c.600-605AD. By now the Caucasus was under stronger Iranian than Romano-Byzantine military influence. At the same time early Byzantine armies themselves reflected considerable Sassanian and Central Asian Turkish influence. The long-sleeved cloak or coat was already a symbol of the military elite, as it long had been within the Sassanian Empire. Here Stephanos I, ruler of the central Georgian region of Iberia, kneels before Christ. His head-covering has been damaged but his long sleeved coat, fully open down the front, has decorated borders. He also wears thick riding boots. Since Stephanos had been awarded the rank of *patrikios* or "nobleman" by the Byzantines, some aspects of his costume might reflect this status (in situ, Church of the Holy Cross, Mtzkhet'a, Georgia).

B   Demetre Hypatos, Georgian relief-carving c.600-605 AD. Here another Georgian nobleman kneels before Christ. His costume is less decorated than that of Stephanos I but the carving is also less damaged. A large hood-like hat, partially obscured by an angel's hand, covers his head and the side of his face. It is remarkably similar to a surviving 8th century silk-covered hood or hat from the northern slopes of the nearby Caucasus mountains and to those hoods or hats which cover the helmets of almost all Byzantine soldiers in 7th to 9th century AD Byzantine art. Demetre Hypatos either wears shoes over loose leggings or very soft riding boots, much as would be worn in 7th to 10th century Islamic Persia, or maybe he has very baggy trousers tucked into his shoes (in situ, Church of the Holy Cross, Mtzkhet'a, Georgia).

C   Prince Nerseh Kamskaran, Armenian relief-carving c.640 AD. This is one of a series of carvings on the exterior of a church made to celebrate the Armenians' participation in the defeat of Zoroastrian Persia by the Byzantine Emperor Heraclius. Meanwhile the Sassanian Empire was already collapsing before the Muslim Arabs. The Byzantines had already been crushed in Syria and Arab raiders had reached southern Armenia.   Whatever side they took in the final struggle between Byzantium and Sassanian Iran, the Armenians were already equipped, dressed and militarily organized in an Iranian rather than a Roman manner. The figures seen here show the frontality and highly stylized character of Persian Islamic art. For example the exterior of the long-sleeved cloak probably represents stylized fur or sheepskin, such coats being typical of Armenia with its bitter winters until modern times. The pattern on the tunic beneath similarly represents the extravagantly long sleeves adopted by the elite (in situ, Cathedral, Mrèn, Armenia).

D   Prince David Saharouni, Armenian relief-carving c.640 AD.   A second figure on the exterior of Mrèn Cathedral is dressed in the same manner but has a beard and seems to wear a different version of the hat or hood already seen in the Georgian carvings. It appears to be made of three panels and as such was structurally different both to the surviving example from the northern Caucasus and to those seen in Byzantine art. Similar headgear might, however, appear in some slightly later but even more stylized Persian Islamic sources (in situ, Cathedral, Mrèn, Armenia).

E   Armenian relief-carving c.640 AD. Rarely noticed among the carving at Mrèn is a saddled horse. It provides extremely important information at a time and in an area where vital changes were taking place in horse-harness. The bridle and bit are rather confused and apparently damaged, but the saddle clearly has the very raised saddle-bow or pommel seen in other sources. It similarly lacks any raised cantle at the rear and has no stirrups (in situ, Cathedral, Mrèn, Armenia).

F & G Relief carvings, Armenian, said to be early 7th century AD. These figures are hunting rather than involved in warfare. The man on foot thrusts a large spear and wears a very short tunic. The horse-archer offers more information, including what appears to be another version of the hood or hat seen elsewhere. His bow is probably being pulled back using a thumb-draw. His riding boots seem to be drawn up over the knees in a manner which is known to have been brought to Iran from Central Asia by Turkish slave or mercenary troops a century or so later. Along with a deep-seated saddle with raised pommel and cantle, a horse with a knotted tail, decorative collars, a breast-strap but no breeching straps, there are stirrups. These are indicated by a line across the foot and by the horizontal position of the foot itself. All such features strongly suggest that the normally accepted date of this carvings is several centuries too early. Like several other remarkable Armenian and Georgian relief carvings, it is likely to have been made in the 9th or even 10th-11th centuries AD (in situ, exterior of church, Ptghni, Armenia).

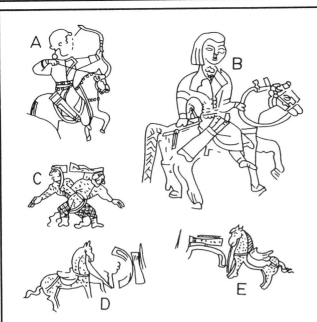

B Partially gilded bronze bowl from Khwarazm, Suhgdian 5th to 8th centuries AD. The region of Khwarazm was once a fertile agricultural delta where the Amu Darya (Oxus) river disgorged into the Aral Sea. Medieval Khwarazm was a rich land of cities and small towns inhabited by a mixed Iranian and Turkish population. It remained so until devastated by the Mongols and then destroyed by ill-conceived Soviet irrigation schemes. The figure on this fine bronze bowl wears the double-breasted tunic with large revers characteristic of the Sughdian military aristocracy. His only visible weapons are a bow just visible behind his left hip and the arrows in a large box-like forward-facing quiver on his right hip. He still has no stirrups, which suggests that the bowl was made closer to the 5th than to the 8th century. His saddle can barely be seen but is secured by both a breast and breeching straps. The details of the bridle and bit cannot be identified but the horse's mane retains the trimmed tufts that, having been seen for many hundreds of years, would fall from favour after the coming of Islam (State Hermitage Museum, St. Petersburg, Russia).

C - E Engraved decoration on the rim of a silver bowl found in the Ural Mountains, probably Khazar 6th century AD. The Turkish Khazars never formed part of the Sassanian Empire and were, in fact, more inclined to support Byzantium in its wars against the Persians. Nevertheless they clearly had an influence upon, and were perhaps influenced by, Sassanian border regions north of the Caucasus. This silver bowl, which is only tentatively identified as Khazar workmanship, is decorated with two figures (C) between two horses and piles of weaponry (D & E). The men are dressed in relatively tight-fitting tunics, decorated baggy trousers and soft riding boots. They wear low hats, one with a turban-like cloth. The simply drawn weaponry consists of curved bowcases of the type designed to take unstrung bows, box-like quivers and perhaps swords. The horses have fully developed framed saddles with raised pommels in front and cantles behind, breast and breeching straps but no visible stirrups. The latter were, however, certainly known in the western steppes where the Khazars built their powerful state (State Hermitage Museum, St. Petersburg, Russia).

28. The Borderlands: Transoxania. The great majority of new military fashions, techniques and technologies entering Iran during the Sassanian Empire came across the northeastern frontier in Transoxania. Ultimately they originated in Turkish Central Asia or even China. The preceding Parthian rulers of Iran came from this area and the last century of the Sassanian Empire saw another very powerful wave of such influences. While they can be found in the art of the Sassanian heartlands to the south and west, they are naturally easier to see in the art of Transoxania itself.

A Glazed decoration on a damaged ceramic pot from Marw, Turkmenistan, Sassanian or Suhgdian, 4th or 5th centuries AD. The most striking features are the use of the thumb-draw, the size and outline of the saddle and above all the large open-ended quiver hanging at an angle from a belt-strap on the man's right hip. This is a form more typical of settled rather than nomadic horse-archers, but is more advanced than those seen further west in the Sassanian Empire (State Hermitage Museum, St. Petersburg, Russia).

The most important such army was that of the Arab Lakhmids who had their capital at Hira, not far from the river Euphrates. Other powerful Arab tribes had dominated the desert frontier before the Lakhmids, who may have been of south Arabian origin, arrived in the 3rd century AD. From then on the Sassanians supported the Lakhmids in return for the latters' loyalty in defending the settled areas of Iraq from other Arab raiders. One of the first Lakhmid rulers was Imru'l Qays whose long reign stretched into the 4th century. The military system he developed was based upon the Sassanians with a close-knit ruling famil and a well-organized army. The Lakhmid capital a Hira consisted of a brick-walled compound containing a large two-storey palace or fort. It was a famil rather than tribal centre where the Lakhmid ruler relied on foreign or mercenary troops. A mercenar elite formed a personal guard and a garrison whil the Lakhmids rarely employed tribal forces, thoug they did recruit from subject tribes on an individu: basis. Many Lakhmid troops were well-armoured i mail but the best equipped were probably the *wada*

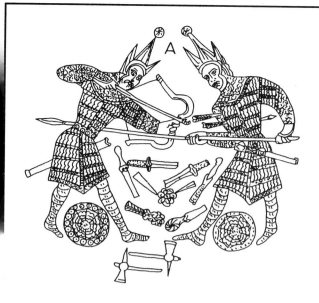

29.   The Borderlands: Khurasan.

A   Gilded silver plate from Kulagysh, Sassanian Khurasan 7th or early 8th centuries AD. This is one of the most magnificent among many examples of metalwork produced in or near the north-eastern regions of the Sassanian Empire. The peculiar headgear of its two warriors find their closest parallels in 9th or 10th century AD ceramics from Islamic Khurasan. The figures probably represent mythical heroes, possibly connected with Zoroastrian festivals marking the cycle of seasons. As such their three-pointed headgear may have had a symbolic meaning rather than reflecting real helmets. The rest of their very detailed military equipment appears to be entirely realistic. Hanging from the rim of the perhaps symbolic headgear is a large mail aventail to protect neck and shoulders. A long cuirass, clearly of lamellar construction and opening down the front, also has small sleeves. Since it would be impossible to make lamellar sleeves flexible enough to protect the armpit as well as the outside of the arm, these would have been more like shoulder flaps like the lamellar upper-arm defences of the later Mongol period. Beneath their lamellar cuirasses both men have long sleeved mail hauberks. There are also extended flaps, in one case shown as mail with some kind of edging, to protect the back of the wearer's hands. Other representations of such hand-extensions show them to have been of rigid rather than mail construction, so the presence of mail over the right hand of one of these warriors might be an artist's error. It is impossible to state with certainly what covers the men's legs. The pattern recalls that shown in earlier Sassanian art and which could be interpreted as padded or quilted leggings. But laminated leg armour of bronze or hardened leather strips is clearly shown on 7th to 9th centuries art from nearby Transoxania, though this does not extent above the knees nor over the feet. Perhaps the artist who made the plate was trying to portray a new form of laminated leg armour which he did not fully understand. Relatively short straight scabbards hang at an acute angle from the warriors' belts, one clearly being suspended by straps to a pair of D-shaped attachments. This was a new method of hanging a scabbard, at least as far as the Sassanians were concerned. Again it was of Central Asian or perhaps Chinese origin. The straight swords from these scabbards lie broken between the warriors, one blade having the narrowed or "waisted" outline characteristic of Indian swords rather than those from Central Asia. Other broken or abandoned weaponry includes two short-hafted axes, two small shields, and the fragments of what might have been elaborate maces. Meanwhile the two warriors continue their combat with a spear, bow and arrows (State Hermitage Museum, St. Petersburg, Russia).

B   Reconstruction of Khurasani heavily armoured warrior based on the silver gilt plate from Kulagysh in the Hermitage.

a unit of 1,000 Sassanian *aswaran* cavalry sent on rotation by the King of Kings.

These forces owed allegiance to the Lakhmid ruler rather than the amorphous Lakhmid state and were "inherited" by his successor, a concept as yet alien to the independent-minded bedouin. The Sassanian Emperor also gave the Lakhmid elite estates comparable to those of the Iranian *dihqans*, though they were of inferior quality around the edges of the cultivated zone.

As far as the Sassanians were concerned the primary function of their Lakhmid vassals was to control the Arabian tribes. To do this the Lakhmids played one tribe off against another in an ever-changing kaleidoscope of alliances. Senior tribesmen were kept as honoured "hostages" and if the tribes resisted Lakhmid tax gathers they would be raided. Long distance expeditions were normally only carried out in alliances with other tribes and Lakhmid military power fluctuated considerably, often reflecting the fortunes of their Sassanian overlords.

Within Iraq the Lakhmid ruler enjoyed great influence at the Sassanian Court. King Mundhir, for example, was military tutor to the future Bahram V and later gave him vital support in his struggle against rebellious nobles. During the 5th century the Lakhmids appear to have taxed, and thus to some extent controlled, distant Oman on behalf of the Sassanian Empire. The 6th century Lakhmid King

30. **The Borderlands: Sughdia.** The lands between the Amu Darya (Oxus) and Syr Darya (Jaxartes) rivers were rich and highly civilized during the early Middle Ages. Known as Transoxania to the ancients and Mawara al Nahr "Beyond the River" to the Muslims, this area flourished as a staging post in the Silk Road between the Middle East and China. Over the past half century archaeologists have uncovered numerous well preserved wall paintings illustrating the courtly life, culture and warfare of the sophisticated Sughdian civilization (State Hermitage Museum, St. Petersburg, Russia).

A   Wall painting from Room VI/41 in the great palace at Panjikent near Samarkand, Sughdian 7th or early 8th centuries AD. A hunting scene shows a horseman using a lassoo. He has no hat, his hair apparently blowing in the breeze, but he wears a tight-fitting coat with large decorative shoulder panels and a broad decorated hem. On his left hip, apparently hanging from a single belt, are a very long but straight sword with an angled "sabre" grip and a long bowcase containing two unstrung bows. He clearly uses a stirrup and sits deeply in a saddle which has a raised saddle-bow or pommel at the front. Most of the horse's bridle has been lost in this faded picture but its bit is of the framed metalic caveson type.

B   Wall painting from Reception Hall VI/1 in the great palace at Panjikent near Samarkand, Sughdian 7th or early 8th centuries AD. Among many combat scenes on the Panjikent wall-paintings is this fragment showing two fully armoured men fighting on foot with a smaller standard bearer standing between them. Similarities with the gilded silver plate from Kulagysh are obvious and there are also close parallels between the arms and armour in these sources. But there are significant differences. The helmet on the left is a segmented framed form with a pointed finial and other decorations. It is secured by a perhaps laminated chin-strap. This is also visible on the right-hand figure whose face is clearly protected by a long nasal. Both men have mail aventails to cover their necks and shoulders, plus mail hauberks with three-quarter length sleeves. These mail armours, which are shown reaching to the knees in other wall-paintings, are worn beneath large lamellar cuirasses extending from mid-chest to shins. Both lamellar cuirasses consist of a piece to protect the upper body and two larger sheets forming skirts which open down the front. The artist has taken pains to show two different forms of lamellar construction, perhaps indicating bronze or iron in one case, larger lamellae of hardened leather in the other. Archery equipment includes a large recurved bow almost certainly of composite construction, a long box-like quiver worn on the right hip and an even longer slender bowcase for an unstrung bow on the left hip.

C   Wall painting from Room VI/41 in the great palace at Panjikent near Samarkand, Sughdian 7th or early 8th centuries AD. The paintings in this part of the palace were found in a remarkable state of repair and still rose to a considerable height up the wall which consisted of several rows of continuous pictures rather like strip-cartoons in a child's comic book. The figures shown here came from the defeated army which formed one half of a battle scene. All the cavalrymen have pointed helmets of segmented construction with short nasals and held in place by broad chin-straps. Three include face-covering mail aventails, two having aventails that only cover the neck, one of which seems to be fabric-covered as no mail is indicated. The man furthest away clearly wears no other layer over his mail hauberk while the closest figure even more clearly has a front opening tunic over his mail hauberk. The only other defences are three relatively small round shields carried high on the left arms. Nevertheless several other paintings from Panjikent clearly include laminated arm and leg defences. Beneath his coat and presumably also his mail hauberk the closest figure has a long-sleeved shirt, the right sleeve of which has been thrown to its full extent as the man falls from his horse. His riding boots are tight-fitting, apparently slit or sewn up both the inside and the outside of the leg, and with pointed toes. The saddle is again of the large deep almost modern form with a decorated breast strap but no breeching strap. The closest horse also appears to be the only animal in this particular picture to have a framed caveson bit with extended cheek pieces making it, in effect, a form of curb bit.

Mundhir fought the Romans and their Ghassanid Arab vassals in Syria, as well as the Kinda tribe in an effort to re-establish Lakhmid control over central Arabia. Khusru I may even have appointed Mundhir as ruler of Oman, Bahrayn and Yamamah (these covering the entire southern coast of the Gulf), as well as the Hijaz in western Arabia. By 530 AD Lakhmid control extended to Najran on the borders of Yemen., but around 600 AD Khusru II overthrew the Lakhmids, executing their last king Nu'man III, and garrisoned the area with regular troops. It was a disastrous mistake and only a generation later the Sassanian defenders of the desert frontier failed totally against invading Muslim Arabs.

The Lakhmids were not, of course, the Sassanians' only vassals in Arabia. The relationship between the Empire and pre-Islamic Arabia is little understood, though it is clear that the Sassanians preferred to support settled Arab dynasties of "noble" status rather than powerful bedouin groups as the Romans and Byzantines tended to do. In addition to the Lakhmids they offered their protection to the Julanda of Oman and the Banu Hanifah in what is now eastern Saudi Arabia. During the 6th century such rulers were bolstered by Sassanian garrisons and it is worth noting that the proud Banu Hanifah put up the strongest resistance to Muslim domination anywhere within the Arabian peninsula.

31. The Borderlands: Khotan. The region immediately east of the Pamir mountains never fell within the Sassanian Empire although its people spoke an Iranian language. Here modern China, Pakistan, Afghanistan and the newly freed states of what had been Soviet Central Asia meet in the high peaks of the Pamirs and Hindu Kush. During the early Middle Ages the princes and warriors of this area were often caught up in great military events which swirled around the fluid eastern frontiers of the Sassanian Empire. The last shadowy claimant to the Sassanian throne seems to have attempted a last ditch resistance, supported by the Chinese, in these high mountains in the 7th century.

A Fragment of a ceramic figurine from Ak-Terek, Khotan, 1st to 3rd centuries AD. Once wrongly identified as "a monkey riding a camel", this figurine portrayes an armoured man riding an armoured horse. Both armours would have been of lamellar construction. Clearly no stirrups are being used but a deep seated saddle is visible (British Museum, London, England).

B Incised design on a gemstone from Yoktan, Khotan 2nd or 3rd century AD. This figure has been described as a warrior of "Indo-Scythic type". In fact he is a typical heavily armoured horse-archer as might have been found in many parts of eastern or western Turkestan, Iran and Afghanistan. His abundant weaponry includes a spear in his right hand, an axe or mace in his left, an apparently curved sabre hanging from his belt, a quiver and a bowcase containing a strung bow. Such a bowcase could suggest a slightly later date for this gemstone. He is probably wearing a lamellar cuirass with short flap-like sleeves, a segmented helmet and an aventail. This latter piece of armour seems to go over, rather than to hang from, the rear of his helmet. Its closest parallels may be found in 12th and 13th century Turkish helmets in Islamic art (British Museum, London, England).

C Stucco statuette, Tang China possibly 7th century AD. This tomb guardian warrior figure has been identified as a "Tocharian soldier". His costume and armour are certainly different from that of ordinary Chinese warriors of this period. The Tocharians were an eastern Iranian people inhabiting the Pamir Mountains and they appear to have served as professional soldiers as well as caravan guards far beyond their homeland. The most notable feature of this figure is a large hood-like hat with a tuft on top. It may have been worn over a helmet and it recalls similar, though generally smaller, hoods worn over helmets by other Iranian peoples further west. The thick shoulder-covering pieces of presumed felt or buff leather are, however, closer in style to Chinese equipment while the extravagantly long sleeves of his coat could be found in China, Turkish Central Asia or Sassanian Iran (Nelson-Atkins Gallery, Kansas City, USA).

Yemen in the deep south had its own separate, wealthy and sophisticated civilization thousands of years old; nor was pre-Islamic central Arabia as poor or backward as once thought. Archaeologists have yet to find a complete new civilization as they did in Transoxania, but they have uncovered fortified commercial towns and tribal capitals decorated with fine wall-paintings, metalwork and other craftsmanship. Early Islamic records describe some tribal elites dressed in silk finery, perfumes and jewels like the Persians. Nor was Sassanian interest only defensive. By the late Sassanian period most long distance trade through this area went by sea rather than overland, yet places like Oman had rich trading contacts with East Africa as well as India.

Oman may have fallen under some kind o[f] Sassanian control as early as the reign of the firs[t] King of Kings, Ardashir. Arab legends state that h[e] conquered the entire Gulf coast and slew an Oman[i] king who was a Himyarite; in other words a sout[h] Arabian from Yemen. Lakhmid control of Oman wa[s] probably very tenuous but by the late 6th century [a] large Sassanian garrison under its own *marzban* wa[s] stationed near Suhar to guard the route to Yemen with a political advisor being based inland at Nizw[a] to keep an eye on the local Julanda vassals.

Further west, in the Hijaz region along the Re[d] Sea coast, there seems to have been some degree [of] Sassanian-Lakhmid control over Yathrib (later t[he]

32. The Borderlands: India. The political, military and cultural connections between the eastern provinces of the Sassanian Empire and India are not yet fully understood, but were clearly important. At times the Sassanian frontier ran along the Indus river and included most of what is now Pakistan. In fact the Punjab region served as a bridge between the civilizations of India and Iran as well as China and Turkish Central Asia.

A Cave wall painting, Ajanta, north-central India late 5th century AD. Although this part of India never came under Sassanian rule, the wall paintings in the Ajanta caves include several figues as well as horse-harness and an ocean-going ship that seem to be Sassanian. The cave-paintings may similarly include topics from the south of India, from a civilization almost as far from Ajanta as were the Sassanians. In fact these magnificent Buddhist pictures clearly demonstrate how people and ideas were moving over great distances within southern Asia during the early medieval period. This particular seated figure almost certainly represents a visiting foreign worshipper or pilgrim and has tentatively been identified as a Persian. But his fur brimmed hat, decorated belt, the bands around his upper sleeves so similar to the dedicatory *tiraz* bands of medieval Islamic costume, as well as his long-hilted sword, all make him look more like one of the Turkish military elite from Afghanistan or even Transoxania, both of which areas were largely Buddhist at the time. In addition he holds a shallow bowl in a manner which had precise hierarchical meaning in Central Asian Turkish art (in situ, Cave 1, Ajanta, India).

B Relief carving on a stone door jamb, Gandharan 3rd century AD. The ancient kingdom of Gandhara in north-western Punjab and the foothills of Afghanistan straddled the main trade and cultural routes between India and Central Asia. For many centuries its art also reflected the fact that the area had been ruled by Alexander the Great's successors. Whereas Gandharan portrayals of the dominant military elite show men dressed and equipped in a rather Iranian and Central Asian manner, ordinary warriors look much more Indian. This small figure of an infantry archer, for example, has his hair tied up in a top-knot and only seems to wear loose trousers or a loin-cloth. His bow is of a simple construction and was almost certainly made from a single stave of wood or bamboo like the traditional bows of India (Museum of Fine Arts, Boston, USA).

C Carved stone relief panel, Gandhara 3rd century AD. The somewhat disproportionately represented mahout or elephant driver on this carving has two interesting features. The first is the curved elephant goad with which he controlled the animal. It is virtually identical to surviving elephant goads from over a thousand years later. The second is a clearly illustrated turban tied at the side of his head and running beneath his chin. Turbans were not a characteristic of the Persians or early Arabs but were adopted by the latter during their conquest of Afghanistan and the frontier regions of India. In other words this form of turban, as shown in Gandharan art, would probably have been the type which become fashionable among the Muslim Arabs five hundred years later (Museum of Fine Arts, Boston, USA).

become known as Medina, the second most sacred city of Islam) in the late 6th century. Other parts of the strategic Hijaz were dominated by Jewish Arab tribes who tended to be anti-Byzantine and pro-Sassanian as a result of Christian persecution of Jews elsewhere. These Jewish Arab tribes are recalled in early Islamic histories as being both warlike and very rich in weapons, perhaps as a result of Sassanian connections. It is also interesting to note that in the 10th century, armours made in Iraq, the Gulf region, Oman and Yemen were regarded as heavier and stronger than those of the Byzantines. This was probably also true back in the 6th and 7th centuries, and could have reflected the Sassanian military heritage.

Of greater significance was the development of the superb Arabian breed of horse during this period. Horses reached southern Arabia very late in history, perhaps the 2nd century AD, but the African Dongola breed seems to have arrived in Yemen via Abyssinia by the 4th century. According to local tradition, the Arab horse originated in eastern Arabia close to the Gulf coast, whereas scientific evidence suggests that the Dongola horse may have interbred

33.   The Borderlands: Afghanistan. At various times the oft changing eastern frontiers of the Sassanian Empire included much of what is now Afghanistan. The people of this area were predominantly Iranian under a Turkish ruling elite. But many were also Buddhist or Hindu and their cultural links with India were almost as strong as their links with Persia. When the Sassanian Empire collapsed before the Muslim Arabs in the 7th century, many aspects of Sassanian military heritage survived in this region for another century.

A   Carved detail from an idol of Surya, from Kotal Khair Khaneh, Sassano-Kushan, 4th or 5th centuries AD. This carving was found not far from Kabul in Afghanistan, but its style is very Indian. On the other hand it includes a horse with an excellent top view of a type of saddle seen in many Sassanian and neighbouring sources. The raised and apparently thickly padded saddle-bow or pommel is very pronounced while the lack of any comparable raised cantle at the back is equally obvious. The seat appears to be quilted and is secured by a broad girth, a broad breast-strap and a much narrower breeching strap beneath the horse's tail (Archaeological Museum, Kabul, Afghanistan).

B - D Silver bowl from Bactria, Sassano-Kushan or Kidarite, late 4th to 6th centuries AD. This beautifully decorated bowl was probably made in what is now northern Afghanistan which, though still largely Buddhist, was under stronger Central Asian influence that the Kabul area. The horsemen shown here may represent members of a dominant warrior aristocracy of Hunnish origin. The vigorous manner in which they are shown is more Turkish than Iranian but certain details show a clear Sassanian connection. These include the shoulder ribbons of one man (B), the boot or shoe ribbons of two others (C & D) and the large tassel-like objects attached to the saddle of the third (D). A large open-ended quiver of this third figure, and the fact that neither of the others has any form of bowcase on his left hip, all point to an Iranian rather than a Central Asian technique of horse-archery. The saddles have raised saddle-bows or pommels, as in the carving from Kotal Khair Khaneh, and two of the bits appear to be of curb form. The two bridles with these curb bits have, perhaps significantly, broadened nose bands such as were seen in the heartlands of the Sassanian Empire. It is also worth noting one other minor feature of one saddle (C) which is the apparent dividing of the breeching strap just behind the saddle. This is a rare characteristic but one that is seen on a late or post-Sassanian carved stucco panel from central Iran. In addition to their large recurved composite bows of angled form, two of these huntsmen have very large straight swords with extravagantly long hilts. Such weapons were characteristic of Central Asia

for some centuries and might ultimately have been of Chinese inspiration. It is, however, also possible that such massive weapons were a Sassanian Iranian development which spread eastwards, eventually being adopted in China. The last Sassanian cavalry forces were noted for the length of their swords, at least in comparison to those of their Arab and Byzantine foes, and extremely large "saddle swords" would be carried as secondary weapons by some Muslim Persian cavalry for many centuries. Here, however, the scabbards for these huge swords are hung from the riders' belts rather than being attached to their saddles (British Museum, London, England).

E - I Wall paintings from Buddhist cave monasteries and temples, Bamyan valley, east Sassanian 6th or 7th centuries AD. The wall-paintings of this part of central Afghanistan were made just before or perhaps shortly after the collapse of the Sassanian Empire. The military equipment worn by various Buddhist deities and heroic figures is an interesting mixture of Iranian, Indian and Central Asian features. It also combines contemporary reality with elements of ancient Indian tradition. One representation of the Sun deity (E) has long hair and a long coat which opens fully down the front like that of a Turkish prince. The long sword with an angled grip hangs in a scabbard from what might have been intended as an old-fashioned scabbard-slide. In contrast another representation of the Sun or Mood deity (F) includes several highly realistic details. The most striking is a relatively short mail hauberk being worn beneath a short shirt. The armour is slit at the front for comfort when riding. In his right hand the deity carries what seems to be a large fluted mace while his left hand grasps the hilt of a typical late Sassanian sword. This is carried in a highly decorated scabbard with two D-shaped suspension points almost identical to those which appear on early 7th century carved rock reliefs far to the west. Similar swords with sometimes very prominent horizontal quillons of almost medieval European form are carried by several other deities (G & H). Archery equipment is given to a "hunter king" (I) in another wall painting. It is of particular interest because the bow is of a very advanced form, having the regularly recurved outline normally associated with the medieval Seljuk Turkish bow rather than the earlier angled form seen in most Sassanian art. This, along with various other minor details, could suggest that the Buddhist wall-paintings of the Bamyan valley were made at a rather later date than has so far been believed (Archaeological Museum, Kabul, Afghanistan).

J   Reconstruction of a Sassano-Kushan warrior huntsman based on the Bactrian silver bowl in the British Museum.

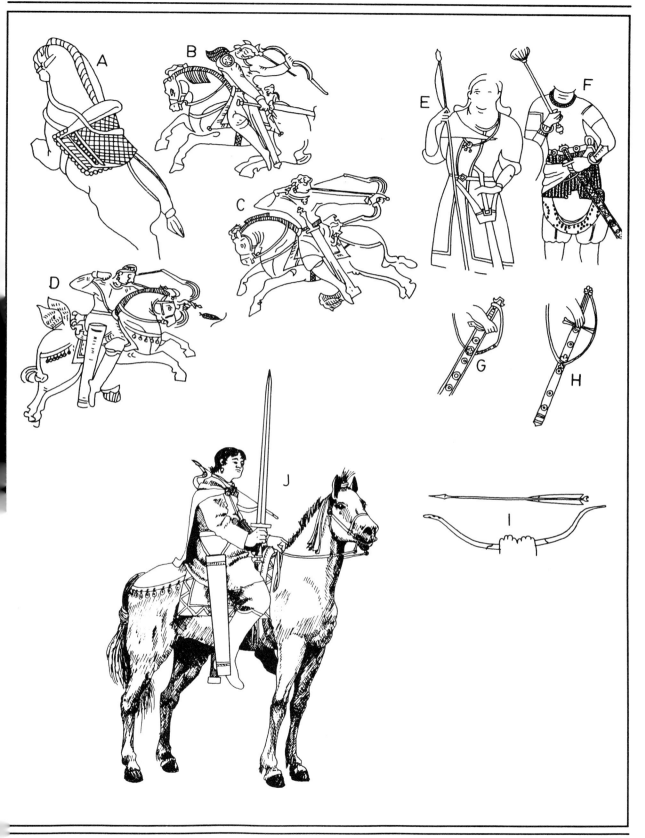

A B C D E F G H I J

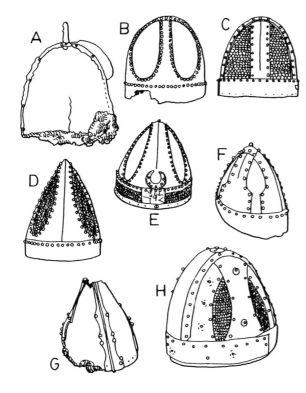

34. Helmets.

A Two-piece iron helmet from Dura Europos, Sassanian mid-3rd century AD. This helmet is made of two large elements joined by a strip of iron from front to back. I has a spike on top, presumably for a plume or other decoration, and a vertical comb, part of which has been lost. The helmet also had decorative "eyebrows" to which a nasal was probably attached. The remains of a mail aventail fastened directly to the rim can also be seen around the bottom the helmet. This particular piece of armour was found on the body of a soldier who had been killed in one of the assault mines beneath the walls of Dura Europos (Yale University Art Gallery, New Haven, USA).

B Framed helmet of "Parthian Cap" shape from Nineveh, Sassanian 4th or 5th centuries AD. Several helmets were found at this Sassanian military post outside Mosul in northern Iraq. Most were relatively undecorated compared to helmets taken from burial sites in northern Iran so perhaps they were worn by ordinary soldiers. Most Sassanian helmets are of this "Parthian Cap" style which has a tall rounded shape when seen from the side, and a pointed outline when seen from the front with two basic plates rivetted to a substantial metal frame. In this example the frame and broad rim-band appear to be made from one large sheet cut and bent over the two basic halves of the helmet (British Museum, London, England).

C Helmet from Cheragh Ali Tepe in northern Iran, Sassanian 5th to 7th centuries AD. This helmet has a simpler construction but is highly decorated, the basic segments or sections having a scale-like surface. In addition the helmet's brow-band has a small crescent-shaped piece of more precious metal attached at the front (Porte de Hal Museum, Brussels, Belgium).

D Helmet from Nineveh in northern Iraq, Sassanian 5th to 7th centuries AD. One of the few decorated helmets from northern Iraq combines the structure and the decorative system of the two preceding example. Here it is seen from the front to show its pointed shape (National Museum, Baghdad, Iraq).

E Helmet from western Iran, Sassanian 6th or 7th centuries AD. This is one of the most decorated surviving Sassanian helmets, yet its "Parthian Cap" structure remains essentially the same. Here, as in other helmets dating from the late Sassanian period, the basic shape is slightly lower and is also less pointed when seen from the front (Römische Museum, Mainz, Germany).

F Helmet from Nineveh in northern Iraq, Sassanian 6th or 7th centuries AD. Another example of a late Sassanian helmet from the military outpost at Nineveh is of mixed construction, the iron plates having been covered in a thin sheet of bronze which would protect them from corrosion and could also be polished. It is still basically a "Parthian Cap" shape but now has an additional small rectangular plate where the frame elements meet on top. The rivets have also been enlarged as a new form of decoration (British Museum, London, England).

G Helmet from Nineveh in northern Iraq, late Sassanian or early Islamic early 7th century AD. One completely new form of helmet was found at Nineveh, clearly derived from the pointed segmented helmets of Central Asia. It could be very late Sassanian or early Islamic since this period saw a huge wave of Turkish Central Asian military influence in the Middle East. This particular helmet is again of mixed iron and bronze construction, four pointed segments being held together by decoratively shaped vertical strips. There is no band around the rim but here there are the remains of a mail aventail fastened directly to the bottom of the helmet. The top of the helmet is missing, perhaps indicating that it was made from a separate piece (British Museum, London, England).

H Helmet from unknown site in Iran, Sassanian 6th or 7th centuries AD. One of the most unusual late Sassanian helmets is made of more pieces than usual. It may have been repaired following battle damage to be re-used by lower grade troops. This might also be suggested by the inferior workmanship of the outer frame and brow-band (County Museum of Art, Los Angeles, USA).

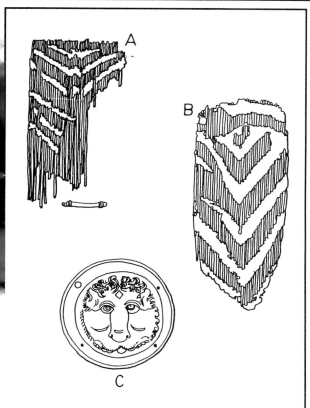

35. Shields.

A & B Two infantry shields or mantlets found in the ruins of Dura Europos, probably Sassanian or Arab ally, mid-3rd century AD. Both these shields are made from vertical canes threaded through strips of untanned leather. They would have been held on the inside by a short grip made from a thicker cane, one of which survived though separated from its shield. Comparable shields are shown in the famous wall paintings from the Dura Europos synagogue. Altogether they represent a simple form of protection made on the spot, which had probably been used by Middle Eastern peoples for thousands of years and would continue to be used for many more centuries (Yale University, Art Gallery, New Haven, USA).

C Silver shield-boss, Sassanian 4th century AD. At the other end of the military scale is this magnificent shield-boss which was surely used by an elite cavalryman or senior officer. It would have been attached to a wood or leather shield, probably round or oval, by four rivets, one of which remains. It is also interesting to note that on the so-called "David Plates", a large collection of silverware made to celebrate the Byzantine Emperor Heraclius' victory over the Sassanians early in the 7th century, Goliath carries a shield with an identical lion-faced boss. Goliath probably represented the Sassanian commander slain by Heraclius who, in turn, was seen as the "David" of his day (British Museum, London, England).

with Persian-type animals in central and northern Arabia. Whatever the truth the Arab horse was clearly known by the 7th century AD.

The most isolated part of the Sassanian Empire was Yemen which came under direct rule in the 6th century. This wealthy part of Arabia had close trading associations with India and cultural links with Iran. Society was dominated by *kabir* clan chiefs, *kail* princes and *satrap* provincial governors based on the old Achaemenid Persian model. A hereditary but non-noble class of warriors dominated Yemeni armies and the land was dotted with fortresses. From the 4th to 5th centuries AD Yemen was the dominant power in Arabia. Yet it remained a fragmented and warlike region whose full military potential would not be recognized until the early Muslim centuries. Even so Yemeni forces reached the Sassanian frontier and possibly raided Iran itself by land and sea in the early 4th century. One echo of these almost forgotten wars tells how a Yemeni army attacked Yamamah, whose rulers were probably already Sassanian vassals. The Yemeni warriors advanced beneath camouflage made of tree branches in a manner recalling Shakespeare's story of "The Forest of Dunsinane" in his play Macbeth.

There was a much stronger Jewish than Christian presence in Yemen in pre-Islamic times. Dhu Nuwas, a powerful southern Arabian ruler in the early 6th century, was himself Jewish Arab and his persecution of Christians prompted the Byzantine Empire to encourage its proxy, the Christian King Kaleb of Abyssinia, to invade Yemen. This, they hoped, would also secure Christian domination of the Red Sea trade route to India. An Abyssinian occupation was followed, in 523/524 AD, by an uprising ; another Abyssinian army being transported to Yemen in Byzantine ships. The Abyssinian general, Abraha, then destroyed the temples of Yemen and tried to attack Mecca to the north with its famous sanctuary, the Ka'aba (subsequently the centre of Muslim worship after being purged of pagan associations). In this campaign Abraha was helped by the pro-Byzantine, anti-Sassanian Kinda tribe of central Arabia.

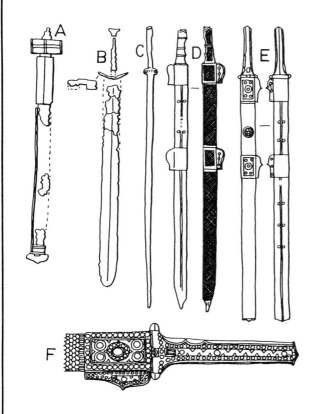

B   Sword from Oman, probably Sassanian 4th to 7th centuries AD. This double-edged sword has a blade with much the same proportions as the fragmented example from Germany, though it appears to be larger. The very damaged guard or quillons are similar to other early medieval swords from the Iranian area, though this style is likely to have had a Chinese origin. On the other hand the flared flat-topped pommel is mirrored in early medieval Indian art. The whole weapon might have been around 82 cms long, which would make it comparable to the largest shown in Sassanian art (Ministry of Culture, Muscat, Oman).

C   Sword from Aphrodisias, western Turkey, probably Sassanian late 6th or early 7th centuries AD. One of the most extraordinary swords ever found is this huge single-edged weapon with a slender blade and a similarly large integral hilt. It is approximately 1.8 metres long and may have been more of a symbolic object than a fighting sword. On the other hand swords almost a tall as a man are recorded being used by Sassanian cavalry and by later horsemen from the Middle East (Archaeological Museum, Aphrodisias, Turkey).

D   Silver sword hilt and scabbard from western Iran, Sassanian probably 6th or 7th centuries AD. Along with several late Sassanian helmets now in European or American museums are a number of similarly dated and decorated swords, still in their scabbards. This example has a scale or feathered decoration engraved on the outer face of both the scabbard and the grip (right) while the inner face (left) is virtually plain. All these late Sassanian swords have straight, parallel-sided, non-tapering, double-edged blades. This specimen has absolutely no guard or quillons to protect the user's hand (Römische Museum, Mainz, Germany).

E & F Sword with gold-covered scabbard and hilt, from western Iran, Sassanian probably 6th or 7th centuries AD. The most magnificent of these late Sassanian swords was in good enough condition for it to be disassembled and studied in detail. The blade was about 4.5 cms across and some 85 cms long, excluding the hilt. The inner face of scabbard and hilt were again virtually plain while the outer faces were highly decorated with geometric patterns and an overall scale or feather design. This outer pattern is not shown on the entire weapon (E left) but is included in the detail of the hilt (F) (Tenri Sankokan Museum, Tokyo, Japan).

36.   Swords.

A   Scabbard with the remains of a blade and quillons, from a grave at Altlussheim, probably of Sassanian origin mid-5th century AD. Thought found in the grave of a Hunnish or allied German warrior in the middle of Europe, this once magnificent weapon is thought to have been made within the Sassanian Empire. The iron blade was straight and double-edged with a highly decorated, partly gold, rectangular guard or quillons (here shown much simplified). The scabbard was equally magnificent, having a gold sleeve around the upper part attached by a long strip of gold to a large chape (Staatliche Museum, Karlsruhe, Germany).

A Yemeni leader, Sayf ibn Dhi Yazan, now asked the Sassanians for help. The King of Kings was reluctant to send an army so far but eventually ordered 800 disgraced *aswanan* cavalry to Yemen where they might hope to regain his favour. This force arrived by sea, fought its way to the Yemeni capital of Sana'a, installed Sayf ibn Dhi Yazan as a Sassanian vassal then returned home. The Abyssinians promptly returned and killed Sayf, whereupon a Sassanian army came back again, drove out the Africans and remained as occupying force until

the rise of Islam early next century. Their partiall assimilated descendants then accepted Islam an under their leader Fayruz (Peroz) the Daylamit fought for the Muslim cause.

Native Yemeni troops mostly served as infant and included renouned archers by the early 7th centur But the main southern Arabian weapon appears have been a short spear with which a warrior cou both cut and thrust - much like the later Afric *assagai*. Wealthier warriors possessed straight-blade

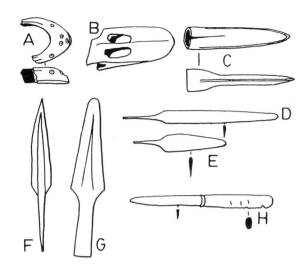

C Spear-blade or foot from Susa, Sassanian 4th century AD. Most probably the butt or foot of a spearshaft, this strangely shaped iron point could have come from an infantry weapon designed to be thust into the ground as a pike, or from a cavalry or infantry spear with points at both ends. The latter idea was certainly common among both the Arabs of Iraq and the Persian-speaking Dailamite infantry of northern Iran only a few centuries later (location unknown).

D & E Dagger blades from Oman, Arab or Sassanian, perhaps 3rd to 7th centuries AD. At first glance these objects look like blunted spear-blades, but they only have a cutting edge down one side. The tangs are, however, round which makes them unusual for daggers. Presumably they were intended to be thust into a hollowed out "plug" grip rather than being sandwiched between the two wooden halves of a grip. Such plug-grip knives were also known rather later in medieval Western Europe (Ministry of Culture, Muscat, Oman).

F Bronze spear or javelin-head from Dura Europos, probably Parthian or Sassanian mid-3rd century AD. Once again a weapon from Dura Europos is made of bronze rather than iron. Its long slender tang suggests that it was a form of javelin thrust into a bamboo haft. Like several apparently primitive weapons found in the ruins of Dura Europos, this bronze blade is more likely to have been used by locally recruited Arab tribal auxiliary troops rather than by the elite imperial forces of either side (Yale University Art Gallery, New Haven, USA).

G Bronze spear-head from Dura Europos, probably Parthian or Sassanian mid-3rd century AD. This perfectly normal spear-head has one very abnormal feature; the tip is rounded and relatively blunt. This is not the result of corrosion as the object is bronze and is otherwise in excellent condition. It would, therefore, not have been an effective thrusting weapon but could have been used for slashing. If so it should be categorized as an early form of staff weapon. Nevertheless, this particular object remains something of a mystery and may, in fact, have been the symbolic top of a standard or flag-pole rather than a fighting weapon (Yale University Art Gallery, New Haven, USA).

H Knife from Shahr-i Qumis, probably Sassanian 6th century AD. Complete weapons with blade and grip intact are rare. This is a very simple single-edged knife which would have been more of a tool than a weapon. The blade is iron, the plug-type grip apparently wood, and there seems to be a small collar or washer between the two (location unknown).

37. Miscellaneous Weapons.

A Bone thumb-ring from Dura Europos, probably Parthian or Sassanian mid-3rd century AD. This broken thumb-ring is one of the earliest such archer's aids yet found. Most others are of non-perishable material such as bronze, silver or in some cases soft carved stone. But their main features remain the same: the ring itself and an extended lip from one side which protects the inside of the thumb. Sometimes there is a stud at the back of the ring, tentatively identified as a "sighting device" to be pressed against the side of the archer's face. Others have a teardrop-shaped stud on the lip of the ring, perhaps to help lock the bowstring as it is pulled back (Yale University Art Gallery, New Haven, USA).

B Bronze axe-head from Dura Europos, Parthian or Sassanian, mid-3rd century AD. Unlike the archer's thumb-ring, which might have been used by Syrian or even Roman troops, this bronze war-axe appears to be a specifically Middle Eastern or Iranian weapon. The fact that it is made of bronze might sound archaic by the 3rd century AD but bronze weapons and, even more commonly, bronze fittings remained in use in this part of the world throughout the Middle Ages, long after they had been almost entirely abandoned in Western Europe. The Middle East was, of course, much poorer in iron resources than Europe. Small war-axes appear in several Parthian and early Sassanian sources and this example, with its open-backed socket and two holes through the blade, would have been lashed to a haft perhaps with rawhide thongs (Yale University Art Gallery, New Haven, USA).

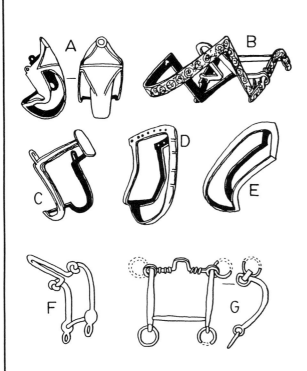

B Bronze curb-bit with integral drop-noseband, Sassanian 3rd to 5th centuries AD. This decorated and elaborate bit incorporated psalions cheek-pieces joined by a rigid crossbar beneath the chin, a large piece which would lie on top of the horse's tongue and a heavy bronze drop-noseband fastened to the upper part of the psalions . This continued to form a bronze strap beneath the mouth. By modern standards it looks a very savage form of bit, but in the hands of an experienced rider it would provide very precise control (Metropolitan Museum of Art, New York, USA).

C Bronze drop-noseband bit from Iran, undated. This incomplete bridle-bit would originally have been much the same as the preceding more decorated example. It includes a plate-like element on top of the drop-noseband which may have spread the pressure exerted on a horse's nostrils when the reins were pulled. Otherwise the only major difference is that the leather straps of the bridle were attached to metal loops at the back of the bridle-bit (private collection).

D Bronze caveson bridle-bit from Susa, Sassanian 4th century AD. A much simpler version of the same kind of caveson as seen above (A), this would have worked in exactly the same manner (present location unknown).

E Iron caveson bridle-bit from Susa, Sassanian 4th century AD. A further even plainer example of a Sassanian caveson bit may have been bent out of shape. Otherwise the upper part, where the nose-band is attached to the piece which runs forward around the front of the animal's mouth, would seem designed to cause great discomfort (present location unknown).

F Iron curb bit from Susa, Sassanian perhaps 4th century AD. This form of curb bit, with its long psalions and substantial tongue piece, would not have been out of place in later medieval Europe. As such it represents the new form of bitting which, possibly developed in Iran rather than in Central Asia, would soon become the norm throughout the settled areas of the Middle East and Europe (present location unknown).

G Iron curb-bit from Tomb B IV at Nouruzmahale, northern Iran, probably late Sassanian undated. Once again a highly developed form of curb bit was found in a presumed late Sassanian context and would not have been out of place in this region over a thousand years later. The reins were attached to large rings at the base of the psalions cheek-pieces while the leather straps of the bridle itself were attached to comparable iron rings at each end of the mouthpiece (present location unknown).

38. Horse-Harness. The Sassanian and preceding Parthian periods saw many changes in equestrian equipment. Not surprisingly several different types of bit have been found by archaeologists.

A Bronze caveson bridle-bit from western Turkey, undated. The largest and most elaborate form of frame-like caveson bridle-bit from the Middle East was found beyond the western frontiers of the Sassanian Empire. It may be a local Roman form or perhaps be earlier or slightly later. Nevertheless it is an excellent example of a very heavy caveson such as those shown in early Sassanian art. The mouthpiece or bit itself is missing (location unknown).

double-edged swords, some reputedly made of Indian steel, and these weapons would be remembered in Arab poetry for many centuries. Yemen had few camels and even fewer horses, yet the great Dhu Nuwas may have fielded a small elite of armoured cavalry even in the early 6th century. Meanwhile the use of war-elephants by their Abyssinian foes almos certainly reflected Sassanian military influence vi the Yemen.

BIBLIOGRAPHY

Original Sources

The Sassanian Empire is one of few great Middle Eastern civilizations to lack its own original historical sources. Fragments of Sassanian writing remain carved on rocks or embedded in later histories and epic tales, most of which were written in Arabic or medieval Persian. Otherwise the historian has to rely on the chronicles of neighbouring and usually hostile cultures such as the Romans. The main sources remain, however, subsequent Islamic histories. For decades Western historians regarded these as extremely unreliabl. Today, however, more detailed scholarship is enabling students of the Sassanian Empire to sift truth, or shadows of truth, from works which were written centuries later as what has been termed "a twilight of historical reality".

Primary Sources

Anon. (trans. E. Sachau), "Die Chronik von Arbela", *Abhandlungen der preussischen Akademie der Wissenschaften* (1915).

Anon. (trans. J. Unvala), *King Kusrav and His Boy* (Paris 1923).

Anon. (trans. J. Mohl), "Modjmel al Tewarikh", *Journal Asiatique*, 3 ser. XI (1841).

Anon. (trans. A. Maricq), "Res gestae divi Saporis", *Syria* XXV 1958).

Al Baladhuri (trans. P.K. Hitti & F.C. Murgotten), *The Origins of the Islamic State*, vol. I (London 1916).

Cassius Dio , *Roman History*, edit. & trans. Cary (London 1954-61).

Firdawsi (trans. R. Levy), *The Epic of the Kings, Shahnama* (London 1967).

Firdawsi (trans. A.G. & E. Warner), *The Shahnama of Firdausi* (London 1905).

Herodianus, *Books I-VIII*, edit. & trans. C.R. Whittaker (Cambridge Mass. 1969-70).

Al Jahiz (trans. Ahmed Zaki Pasha), *Djahiz, le livre de la couronne* (Cairo 1914).

Al Mas'udi (trans. C. Barbier de Maynard & P. de Courteille), *Muruj al Dahab: Les Prairies d'Or* (Paris 1861-77).

Moses Khorenats'i (trans. R.W. Tomson), *History of the Armenians* (Cambridge Mass. 1978).

Al Tabari (edit. I. Yarshater, various translators), *The History of al-Tabari* (New York continuing).

Al Tabari (trans. M.H. Zotenberg), *Chronique de Tabari* (Paris 1867).

Al Th'alibi (trans. H. Zotenberg), *Histoire des Rois des Perses* Paris 1900).

Secondary Sources

Akram, A.I. *The Muslim Conquest of Persia* (Rawalpindi 1976).

Altheim, F. & R. Stiehl (edits), *Die Araber in der Alten Welt* , 5 vols. (Berlin 1964-69).

Austin, N.J.E. *Ammianus on Warfare: An Investigation into Ammianus' Military Knowledge* (Bruxelles 1979)

Balint, Cs. "Vestiges Archeologiques de l'epoque tardive des Sassanides et leur relations avec les peuples des steppes", *Acta Archaeologica Academiae Scientiarium Hungarica*, XXX (1978).

Barisic, F. "Le siege de Constantinople par les Avares en 626", *Byzantion*, XXIV (1954).

Baynes, N.H. "The Military Operations of the Emperor Heraclius", *United Service Magazine* XLVI (1913) & XLVII (1913).

Bivar, A.D.H. "Cavalry Equipment and Tactics on the Euphrates Frontier", *Dumbarton Oaks Papers* XXVI (1972).

Bivar. A.D.H. "Details and 'Devices" from the Sassanian Sculptures", *Oriental Art* V/1 (1959).

Christensen, A. *L'Empire des Sassanides, le peuple, l'état, la cour* (Copenhagen 1907).

Christensen, A. *L'Iran sous les Sassanides* (Copenhagen 1936).

Colledge, M.A.R. *The Parthians* (London 1967).

Cumont, F. "L'uniforme de la cavalerie et le costume byzantins", *Byzantion*, II (1925).

Dain, A. "Saka dans les traites militaires", *Byzantinische Zeitschrift*, XLIV (1951).

David-Weill, J. "Têtes de Chevaux Sassanides", *La Revue des Arts (ex-Musees et Monuments de France)* III (1954).

Downey, G. "The Persian Campaign in Syria in AD 540", *Speculum*, XXVIII (1953).

Dupree, L. "Shamshir Ghar: Historic Cave Site in Kandahar Province, Afghanistan", *Anthropological Papers of the American Museum of Natural History*, XLVI (1958).

The Excavations at Dura-Europos; Preliminary Report of the 6th Season (New Haven 1936): F.E. Brown, "Arms and Armour"; R. du Mesnil du Buisson, "The Persian Mines".

The Excavations at Dura-Europos; Final Report, vol. VIII/1 (New Haven 1956): C.H. Kraeling, "The Synagogue".

Finster, B. & J. Schmidt, *Sasanidische und Frühislamische ruined in Iraq* (Berlin 1976).

Foss, C. "The Persians in Asia Minor and the End of Antiquity", The English Historical Review XC (1975).

Freeman, P & D. Kennedy (edits.), The Defence of the Roman and Byzantine East, British Archaeological Reports, International Series 297, various articles (Oxford 1986).

Frye, R.N. The Golden Age of Persia: The Arabs in the East (London 1975).

Frye, R.N. The History of Ancient Iran (Munich 1984).

Frye, R.N. "Napki Malka and the Kushano-Sasanians", in D.K. Kouymjian (edit.), Near Eastern Numismatics, Iconography, Epigraphy and History (Studies in Honour of George C. Miles) (Beirut 1974).

Frye, R.N. "The Sasanian System of Walls for Defence", in M. Rosen-Ayalon (edit.), Studies in Memory of Gaston Wiet (Jerusalem 1977).

Frye, R.N. "The Turks in Khurasan and Transoxania at the Time of the Arab Conquest", The Moslem World XXV (1945).

Gamber, O. Waffen und Rustung Eurasiens: Fruhzeit und Antike (Brunswick 1978).

Garsoian, N.G. Armenian between Byzantium and the Sassanians (London 1985).

Ghirshman, R. Cinq campagnes de fouilles a Suse (1946-51) (Paris 1952).

Ghirshman, R. Iran: Parthians and Sassanians (London 1962).

Ghirshman, R. "Notes Iraniennes XIII: Trois Epeés Sassanides", Artibus Asiae XXVI (1963).

Ginters, W. Das Schwert der Skythen und Sarmaten in Sudrussland (Berlin 1928).

Gobl, R. Dokumente zur Geschichte der Iranischen Hunnen (Wiesbaden 1967).

Gohlke, W. "Das Geschutzwesen des Altertums und das Mittelalters", Zeitschrift fur Historische Waffen- und Kostumkunde, V-VI (1909-14).

Grancsay, S.V. Arms and Armor: Essays by Stephen V. Grancsay from the Metropolitan Museum of Art Bulletin 1920-1964 (New York 1986).

Grancsay, S.V. "A Sasanian Chieftain's Helmet", Metropolitan Museum of Art Bulletin XXI/5 (Apri 1961).

Gropp, G. Der Gurtel mit Riemenzungen auf den Sasanidischen Reliefs .... Taq-i Bostan", Archaologische Mitteilungen aus Iran, ns III (1970).

Harper, P.O. La Persia nel Medioevo (Rome 1971).

Harper, P.O. (edit.), The Royal Hunter: Art of the Sassanian Empire (New York 1978).

Herrmann, G. "Parthian and Sasanian Saddlery, New Light from the Roman West", Archaeologia Iranica et Orientalis II (1989).

Herzfeld, E. "Firuzabad rock reliefs", Revue des Arts Asiatiques, V (1928).

Huart, C. Ancient Persia and Iranian Civilization (London 1927).

Ingholt, H. Gandharan Art of Pakistan (Peshawar 1968).

Ingholt, H. Palmyrene and Ganharan Sculpture:... (Yale Univ Art Gall, New Haven 1954).

Jettmar, K. Between Gandhara and the Silk Roads, Rock Carvings along the Karakorum Highway, (Mainz 1987).

Joshua Stylites (trans. W. Wright), The Chronicle of Joshua the Stylite (Cambridge 1882).

Kister, M.J. Studies in Jahiliyya and early Islam (London 1980): collection of reprinted articles.

Kondakov, N.P. "Les Costumes orientaux et la cour byzantins", Byzantion, I (1924).

Lieu, S. Rome's Eastern Frontier AD 226-363 (London 1989).

Macuch, R. Studia Semitica necnon Iranica... (Wiesbaden 1989).

McGraw Donner, F. The Early Islamic Conquests (Princeton 1981).

Medinger, L. "L'arc turquois et les archers parthes..." Revue Archeologiques, VI ser, vol II (1933).

Miller, P.A. (trans.), Accounts of Western Nations in the Northern Chou Dynasty (Berkeley 1959).

Modi, J.J. "Archery in Ancient Persia", Journal of the Royal Asiatic Society, XXV (1917-21).

Orbeli, J. Orfevrerie Sasanide (Moscow 1935).

Overlaet, B.J. "Contribution to Sasanian Armament in connection with a decorated helmet", Iranica Antiqua XVII (1982).

Paterson, W.F. "The Sassanids", Journal of the Society of Archer Antiquaries XII (1969).

Peck, E.H. "The Representation of Costume in the Reliefs of Taq-i-Bustan", Artibus Asiae XXXI (1969).

Pope, A.U. "Fortification", in A.U. Pope (edit.), A Survey of Persian Art (London 1939).

Porada, E. The Art of Ancient Iran: pre-Islamic culture (New York 1965).

Potts, D.T. "From Qadi to Mazun, four notes on Oman c.700BC-700AD", Journal of Oman Studies VIII/1 (1985).

Rostovtzeff, M.I. "Le porte-epee des Iraniens et des Chinois", Recueil Th. Uspenskiy (Paris 1930).

Rubin, B. "Die Enstehung der Kataphraktenreiter. im Lichte der Choreszmischen Ausgrabungen", Historia , IV (1955).

Smith, S. "Events in Arabia in the 6th century AD", Bulletin of the School of Oriental and African Studies XVI (1954).

Stark, F. Rome on the Euphrates, the story of a frontier (London 1966).

Sykes, P. A History of Persia, vol. 1, 3rd edition (London 1930).

Thompson, R.C. "The British Museum Excavations in the Temple of Ishtar at Nineveh..." Liverpool Annals of Archaeology and Anthropology, XIX (1932).

Trousdale, W. The Long Sword and Scabbard Slide in Asia (Washington 1975).

Trumpelmann, L. Iranische Denkmaler 6, Iranische Felsreliefs B. Das Sasanidische Felsrelief von Darab (Berlin 1975).

Widengren, G. "Some Remarks on Riding Costume and Articles of Dress among Iranian peoples in antiquity", Studia Ethnographica Upsaliensia II (1956).

Wilkinson, J.C. "The Julanda of Oman", Journal of Oman Studies I (1975).

Yarshater, E. (edit), The Cambridge History of Iran, Volume 3 (1): The Seleucid, Parthian and Sasanian Periods (Cambridge 1983).